in English

1

Third Edition

Teacher's Guide

Michael Walker

Addison-Wesley Publishing Company
Reading, Massachusetts • Menlo Park, California • New York
Don Mills, Ontario • Wokingham, England • Amsterdam • Bonn
Singapore • Sydney • Tokyo • Madrid • San Juan

A Publication of the World Language Division

Contributing Writer: Victoria Thomas

Director of Product Development: Judith Bittinger
Project Director: Elinor Chamas
Editorial: Kathleen Sands Boehmer
Manufacturing/Production: James W. Gibbons
Design: Jeff Kelly
Illustrations: Allan Eitzen, Walter Fournier, Akihito Shirakawa
Art Direction: Publishers' Graphics

ISBN 0-201-53501-7
2 3 4 5 6 7 8 9 10–MU–95 94 93 92

CONTENTS

The Teaching Plans

Communication/Grammar Objectives
Socializing: *greeting, introducing, taking leave*
Inquiring/Reporting: *names/clothing, ownership*
Agreeing/Disagreeing: *yes/no*

simple statements, yes-no/information questions (word order)
verb to be with 3rd person singular
possessive adjectives *my, your, her, his*
demonstrative pronouns *this, that*
contractions *it's, what's, isn't*

Communication/Grammar Objectives
Apologizing
Inquiring/Reporting: *clothing/colors*; *what people are wearing/doing*
Identifying: ages

simple statements, yes-no/alternative/information questions
adjectives (color words)
personal pronouns *he, she, it, they*
questions words *what, who*
contractions *that's, who's, he's, she's, they're*

Communication/Grammar Objectives
Inquiring/Reporting/Identifying: *where things/people are;household furniture/
    rooms; time on the hour/half hour/quarter hour; directions, prices*

simple statements, information questions
prepositions *on, under, in front of, behind, at, in*
personal pronoun *we + are*
time structures (*What time is it?, quarter to/past, half past, It's . . . o'clock.*)
question words *where, when*
contractions *where's, I'm, we're, don't*
definite article *the*

Unit Four

Communication/Grammar Objectives
Reporting: *describing people*
Inquiring/Reporting: *identifying people by what they are wearing; food, likes/ dislikes; prices*

verb *to be* + predicate adjective
pronunciation of [-s], [-z], [-iz] sounds
question words *how old, how much*

Unit Five

Communication/Grammar Objectives
Inquiring/Reporting: *what people are doing; food/drinks, likes/dislikes*

articles *a/an*
plural nouns (count/mass)
present progressive verb forms
pronunciation of [-s] [-z] [-iz] sounds
question words *how many*

Unit Six

Communication/Grammar Objectives
Identifying: *occupations, nationalities, ages, names, books*
Inquiring/Reporting: *quantity*

is/are/am + predicate adjective/predicate noun
singular/plural nouns + *there is, there are*
irregular plural nouns
review of noun plural final sounds [-s], [-z], [-iz]
short answers with *I am, I'm not*

auxiliary verb: *can*
contraction: *can't*
verb: *have to* (*has to*)
prepositions of time *on, in, at*

INTRODUCTION

We're very proud to offer the Third Edition of NEW HORIZONS IN ENGLISH. The First and Second Editions of this series have been extremely successful, and we are indebted to the many teachers and students who have given us valuable feedback and support as they used it. It is partly through this sharing of ideas that we are able to offer another new and improved edition of the series. This edition offers a wide variety of material that meets your needs for structured practice and free production. At the same time, we have been careful to retain all the features of NEW HORIZONS that teachers and students have come to enjoy and rely on in the past. NEW HORIZONS offers success, as always, through its unique blend of **learnability** and **teachability**.

Learnability

The primary needs of the learner—motivation, mastery and a sense of achievement—still characterize the student materials. The books have flair and a spirit of fun, with lessons designed to keep interest high. The content still moves in systematic, small steps, never overwhelming the learner. There is a minimum potential for error in NEW HORIZONS, a maximum potential for easy mastery and extension. A unique step in the learning process is **simultaneous pairwork**. The final step after teacher/class and small group practice, pairwork gives each learner many opportunities for individual practice, and encourages student interaction and teamwork.

The language in NEW HORIZONS is contemporary, relevant English— English that students can and will use outside the classroom. Natural exchanges set in real life contexts grow out of new pages such as Role Play, Partner Practice, and Conversations. In addition, students will enjoy brand new literature pages and an exciting feature called Fast Track that offers students a broader range of language activities, informative readings, research projects, and debates. All students can enjoy these challenging pages without being held accountable for them or tested on them. With NEW HORIZONS, students learn and progress with enthusiasm, moving always to the ultimate goal of communicative competency.

Teachability

We know how important your time is—not only the hours you spend in the classroom, but the hours you spend preparing before class and following up after class. We have tried to make teaching with NEW HORIZONS as easy, effective, and rewarding as possible.

A wide variety of approaches and techniques is utilized in the series—

reflecting the balance between understanding basic structures and *using* those structures in guided and free communication.

Throughout NEW HORIZONS IN ENGLISH you will discover a useful and exciting mix of the following strategies:

- **The Natural Approach**, which allows students to participate and contribute according to their own levels of proficiency.
- **TPR (Total Physical Response)**, which permits students to listen and demonstrate comprehension through their responses to oral commands.
- **The Structural Approach**, which provides an understanding of grammar and builds skills for academic success.
- **The Functional-Notional Approach**, which concentrates on providing students with the language they need and want to communicate.
- **Cooperative Learning**, a strategy through which students learn from one another, participate in partner and group projects, and enjoy meaningful opportunities to practice the language.
- **Content-area Instruction**, with its emphasis on topical readings in subject areas such as science, history, and the environment.

In this guide, objectives, strategies, ways to evaluate and extend the study are clearly presented. Each student page is supported by a detailed, easy-to-follow 3-step teaching plan. Extra information in the form of Predictable Problem notes, Culture Capsules, and references to the audio tape program are supplied as well. Add to these your own favorite ideas and techniques, and you have a series with teachability that can't be matched by any other program.

COMPONENTS AND KEY FEATURES

NEW HORIZONS consists of six levels, moving the learner from zero or false-beginner level of proficiency to advanced. Each level offers a student book, workbook, a teacher's guide, audio cassette tapes, and a placement test.

NEW HORIZONS looks and works even better than before, combining established strengths and appeal with new ideas.

Motivating Student Books

- Artwork that teaches and entertains
- Relevant, useful language
- Systematic small steps to facilitate mastery
- More communicative activities in real life contexts
- Challenging Fast Track strand that broadens the scope of language
- More reading and reading skills development
- More guided discussion and writing practice
- Opportunities for individual practice, pairwork, and free production

Workbooks

- Carefully designed to reinforce and expand the student text
- Test Yourself pages in every unit for continuous self evaluation
- New teacher notes offer suggestions for getting the most out of each page

Innovative Teacher's Guides

- Full-sized student pages supported by creative, 3-step teaching plans
- New student-sized format with spiral binding for easy handling
- Clearly stated and achievable goals spelled out at beginning of each unit
- New reproducible Unit Tests and Song pages
- Review/enrich activities for learners at all levels
- Colored type highlights new vocabulary and structures

Audio Tape Program

- Real contemporary language as it is spoken
- Easy to use in classroom or lab

- Ear-training and sharpening of listening skills
- Development of natural intonation, stress, and rhythm
- Appealing presentation of songs and poems

Related Resources

Your students will also benefit from using the following Addison-Wesley textbooks and visuals, which offer additional practice in the language and skills taught in NEW HORIZONS:

- Lifeskills 1, 2, 3, SECOND EDITION
- Skill Sharpeners 1, 2, 3, 4 SECOND EDITION
- Double Action Picture Cards
- Images Conversation Cards, Sets 1 and 2
- Talk-A-Tivities
- Frontiers

BEFORE YOU BEGIN

Many ideas and teaching strategies appear in this series. The 3-step teaching plans are simple and self-explanatory. Every page can be presented clearly and effectively using the Introduce, Practice, and Follow-Up guidelines. Certain exercises and techniques, however, form the "core" of the series. These give NEW HORIZONS its unique impact and spirit, and deserve special mention.

Key Exercises

1. **Question/answer, short exchanges**. Many of the student pages are designed in a "T-shape" with a model in the shadow box and parallel questions and answers following. Artwork clarifies and cues the text questions and answers. We recommend that students listen, read silently, read aloud, and then practice asking and answering the questions with the type *covered*, using the pictures alone to produce the appropriate questions and answers. Simultaneous **pairwork** (see Key Techniques) should be used with these pages.

2. **Dialogues**. Because the emphasis in NEW HORIZONS is on communication, much of the language is presented in short dialogues, which act as springboards for substitution of structures and/or vocabulary. The substitution items are printed in bold-face (heavy black) type, and are often accompanied by functional artwork. Other dialogues are expanded with only picture cues depicting known patterns and structures. As with the short exchanges, **pairwork** is a very useful final step. For your convenience, new vocabulary is highlighted in blue on the student page reproductions in Guides 1 and 2.

3. **Readings**. Reading texts in the beginning levels are purposely short and tied closely to the oral language presented in each unit. Readings are followed by a variety of question/answer exercises. Pictures and/or picture stories clarify and define the reading content, and are also to be used as non-verbal cues for retelling the reading selections.

   Readings in more advanced levels are purposely longer and represent a fine selection of literary extracts. Depending on the abilities of your students, you may wish to add to the suggestions in the Teacher's Guide by asking comprehension questions about these readings. It is important to employ a **questioning strategy** that leads from the simple to the complex. After assuring that students have comprehended literally, go on whenever possible to ask questions of an inferential and evaluative nature. Help students understand that comprehending is more than "just the facts," and that their opinions are valuable. Asking questions that require such **higher level thinking skills** as inferring, predicting, sequencing, and so on will help students integrate critical thinking with listening, speaking, reading, and writing.

4. **Role Play/Say the Right Thing**. The Role Play page offers conversation practice in real-life contexts. Role Play allows students to practice structures and vocabulary from the lesson, enriched with extra vocabulary presented in a Data Bank. While students are role-playing, monitor them for natural speech patterns. However, do not expect mastery of the conversations. Encourage students to come back to them from other units to practice and review.

    The facing page, Say the Right Thing is a conversational puzzle designed to develop students' awareness of probable and appropriate responses in a natural conversation. Students may work in pairs or groups to discover the two possible conversations and then practice saying them aloud. Finally, they make up similar conversations of their own based on cues provided at the bottom of the page.

5. **Fast Track**. Starting with listening and speaking practice and moving on to reading for information, research projects, and debate topics, Fast Track pages broaden the scope of the language. They offer students challenging activities that stretch their abilities and imaginations without applying the stress of being held accountable.

Key Techniques

1. **Oral Introductions**. This step in the lesson is an important one, and is usually done with books closed. All the different kinds of introductions we suggest share two common purposes: they introduce and review material, and they actively involve the students. The Introduce activities remind students of what they have *already* learned, alert them as to what they are about to learn, and give them more oral practice.

2. **Simultaneous Pairwork**. This unique feature of NEW HORIZONS helps resolve the dilemma of how to give each student maximum opportunities for *individual* oral practice. Pairwork is often the last step in *Practice*, and can be called the "overlearning" stage.

    A large percentage of material in the student books is especially designed for this pairwork. Pairwork has positive values for both students and teachers. As pairs work together, the teacher is released from the front of the room and can move about the classroom, observing, prompting, evaluating, correcting, and *praising* each student's work. The value of pairwork for the students is obvious—they get the opportunities they need to do extra listening and speaking, to support and teach one another, and to use the language as a socializing force.

Be sure students understand exactly what they are to do *whenever* you break up the class into groups and pairs. Observe working pairs carefully. Change pairs during the course, so that students can listen and respond to many different voices.

Pair practice should proceed in the following way. You may not want to use *every* step, but each student should get a chance to ask and listen *at least* once, and to carry out Step 6 (all type covered).

1. Student A reads the questions (or the first dialogue line). Student B reads the answers (or the response).

2. Students switch roles and Repeat Step 1.

3. Students switch again. A reads the questions/cues again. B covers the type and uses the pictures to respond.

4. Students switch and repeat Step 3.

5. Practice with questions/cues covered.

6. Now students cover *both* sides of the text (or all of the dialogue type) and produce appropriate language.

7. Last, pairs should then be able to *expand* the text exercise and produce parallel exchanges or short dialogues of their own.

Objectives

Communication
Socializing: *greeting, introducing, taking leave*
Inquiring/Reporting: *names/clothing, ownership*
Agreeing/Disagreeing: *yes/no*

Grammar
simple statements, yes-no/information questions (word order)
verb to be with 3rd person singular
possessive adjectives *my, your, her, his*
demonstrative pronouns *this, that*
contractions *it's, what's, isn't*

Vocabulary/Expressions

				Data Bank
bathrobe	it	suit	Bye.	briefcase
belt	jacket	sweater	Come again soon.	cane
blouse	my	that	Excuse me.	coat
dress	name	this	Glad to meet you.	pen
friend	no	tie	Good-bye.	purse
hat	raincoat	what	Good morning.	wallet
her	scarf	yes	Hello.	
his	shirt	you	Here you are.	
is	skirt	your	Hi.	
			Pleased to meet you.	
			See you later.	
			So long.	
			Thank you.	
			Thanks.	
			Well . . .	
			You're welcome.	

Introduce the Unit

Do not teach the color names until Unit Two. You can, of course, identify them very quickly if a student asks you to do so.

Have students open their books to page 1 and listen to you **read** (or play the tape for) the short dialogues. They should be able to understand some or all of the meanings of these sentences from the pictures. Some of the students may already know some of the words.

NEW VOCABULARY | NEW STRUCTURE

1 Introduce

1. Point to yourself and say *My name is* . . . . Repeat several times; write the structure with your name on the board.
2. Say to a student *My name is* . . . (that student's name). Have students repeat. Practice with several students.
3. Go around the class practicing in the following manner:

    T: What's *your* name? (Stress *your.*)

    S: *My* name is . . . .
4. Ask a male student:

    T: What's your name?

    S: My name is . . . .

    T: (To the class) *His* name is . . . . (Stress *his.*)

    Have class repeat in **chorus.** Repeat with several students.
5. Repeat the above procedure with a female student.

    T: (To the class) *Her* name is . . . . (Stress *her.*)

2 Practice

1. **Read** (or play the tape for) the dialogue on page 2. Students follow silently. Read again and practice in **chorus**.
2. Write on the board:

    What is your name?   What's your name?   My name is . . . .

    Point out the contraction *what's* and practice in **chorus.**
3. Select a group of four students to demonstrate how you want the students to take turns: Student 1 will ask the other three *What's your name?* Each student will answer. Now student 2 will ask; the others answer. Continue until each student has had a chance to question and respond.
4. Point to a male student and ask *What's his name?* Class replies in **chorus** *His name is* . . . . Repeat the above procedure with a female student.
5. Write both questions and answers on the board:

    What's his name?   His name is . . . .

    What's her name?   Her name is . . . .

3 Follow Up

Divide the class into groups of four. Have one group work in front of the class with your help. The groups work simultaneously.

    S1: My name is . . . .

    What's your name?

    S2: My name is . . . .

    S1: What's his/her name? (pointing to Student 3)

    S2: His/her name is . . . .

1 Introduce

1. Say to a student:

   > **T:** Hello, my name is . . . .
   >   What's your name?
   > **S:** My name is . . . .
   > **T:** Pleased to meet you. (Write on the board.)

   Repeat several times, substituting *glad* for *pleased*.

2. Introduce Student 1 to Student 2.

   > **T:** This is my friend.
   > **S1:**   Pleased to meet you. (Prompt if necessary.)
   > **S2:**   Glad to meet you. (Prompt if necessary.)

   Repeat; practice in groups.

3. Write *Good morning*, *Good-bye*, *So long*, and *See you later* on the board.

2 Practice

1. **Read** (or play the tape for) the dialogue on page 3. Students follow silently. Read again and practice in **chorus**.
2. **Pairwork,** students working at the same time. See **Before You Begin** at the front of this book for complete details.

You may not wish to follow *each* step for each exercise designed for **pairwork**. You *will* want to take advantage of this unique feature as often as possible. It gives students maximum opportunities for oral practice. Listen, model, correct, and praise pairs. Do not worry about the noise level during pairwork practice.

3 Follow Up

1. Have students do **Workbook** page 1.
2. Help students learn how to spell their names by reviewing letters of the alphabet, if necessary. Write on the board *How do you spell your first/last name?* Then while they are practicing introduction, greeting, and leave-taking—here and later on—they can ask each other to spell their first names and/or last names.

Culture Capsule. Greeting and leave-taking customs in the United States are often more informal than those in other cultures. Notice that as Mary and Tom meet informally (page 2), they do not shake hands, even though they are strangers. However, Mary formally introduces Lucy to Tom and, in this case, the two shake hands. The same is true of Mary and Don on page 3. *Hello* is a more formal greeting than *Hi*. Displays of affection, such as embracing and kissing, are limited to family members or very close friends.

THREE/*Unit 1/3*

1. What's his name?

    Ben

    His name is Ben.

2. What's her name?

    Lucy

    Her name is Lucy.

3. What's her name?

    Mary

    Her name is Mary.

4. What's his name?

    Peter

    His name is Peter.

5. What's her name?

    Carmen

    Her name is Carmen.

6. What's his name?

    Mike

    His name is Mike.

7. What's her name?

    Sally

    Her name is Sally.

8. What's his name?

    Don

    His name is Don.

NEW VOCABULARY | NEW STRUCTURE

1 Introduce

(Books closed) Quickly review *What's his/her name?* and *His/her name is . . . .*
Go around the class asking:

       T: What's his/her name?
       C: His/her name is . . . .

Predictable Problem. Some students will have trouble remembering the differences between *his, her,* and *your.* You may want to spend extra time on this. Have students complete this group of three sentences:

       Her name is . . . .
       His name is . . . .
       Your name is . . . .

2 Practice

1. Have students open their texts to page 4. **Read** the entire page slowly (or play the tape).
2. **Read** again and have students answer in **chorus.**
3. **Pairwork** with the questions and answers. Go around the room checking and encouraging pairs.

3 Follow Up

Progress Check. Have pairs of students move around the room greeting and introducing each other. Repeat with leave-taking. Students should be able to produce something like this:

       S1: Hi, what's your name?
       S2: My name is . . . .
            What's your name?
       S1: My name is . . . .
            What's his/her name?
       S2: His/her name is . . . .
            Hi, ... This is my friend . . . .
       S3: Hello, ... Pleased to meet you.
       S2: Hello, ... Glad to meet you.

1 Introduce

(Books closed)

1. Write *Yes, it is.* and *No, it isn't.* on the board. Point to one student and ask another:

   T: Is his/her name . . . ?
   S: Yes, it is./No, it isn't. (Prompt if necessary.)

2. Point out the contraction *isn't* and write *is not* next to the sentence. Ask in the same manner as above:

   T: Is her name . . . ? (Use an imaginary name.)
   S: No, it isn't.

2 Practice

1. **Read** (or play the tape for) the dialogue at the top of the page. Students follow silently in their books.
2. Point out the italicized *is* in the dialogue; remind the class that italicized words get extra stress.
3. **Read** the dialogue again and have the class repeat in chorus.
4. **Pairwork.** Have students work with the entire page. Check intonation and stress as you walk around the room listening, modeling, and praising pairs.

Predictable Problem. The structure *it is* is often a difficult one for some students to master. Students may slide over, or omit entirely, the *it.* Listen carefully as students use this construction; re-model and correct as necessary.

3 Follow Up

1. Have students do **Workbook** pages 2 and 3.
2. If you think students still may not know each other's names, have them print out their name on a piece of paper folded in half so that it stands up on their desk or table. Practice this dialogue with several students individually, then have students do **pairwork** with the conversation.

   T: Hi (wrong name)!
   S: Hi (teacher's name).
   But, my name's not . . . . It's (right name).
   T: I'm sorry. Your name's (right name)?
   S: Yes, that's right.

   Listen to students as they "correct" their partner. If their tone seems too unfriendly, show them how to soften their response.

—Good morning, Tom.
—Good morning, Mary. Is his name John?
—No, it isn't.
—Well, what *is* it?
—It's Fred.

1.
—Is his name Ben?
—Yes, it is.

5.
—Is her name Lucy?
—Yes, it is.

2.
—Is his name John?
—No, it isn't.

6.
—Is her name Susan?
—No, it isn't.

3.
—Is his name Peter?
—No, it isn't.
—Well, what *is* it?
—It's Mike.

7.
—Is her name Carmen?
—No, it isn't.
—Well, what *is* it?
—It's Sally.

4.
—Is his name Don?
—No, it isn't.
—Well, what *is* it?
—It's Jack.

8.
—Is her name Mary?
—No, it isn't.
—Well, what *is* it?
—It's Carmen.

FIVE/Unit 1/5

What's this? **It's a hat.**

hat

scarf

shirt

tie

jacket

raincoat

sweater

blouse

skirt

belt

dress

bathrobe

1. Is this a hat? No, it isn't.

2. Is this a sweater? Yes, it is.

3. Is this a blouse? Yes, it is.

4. Is this a tie? No, it isn't.

5. Is this a shirt?  Yes, it is.

6. Is this a dress?  Yes, it is.

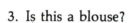
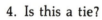

6/Unit 1/SIX

NEW VOCABULARY | NEW STRUCTURE

1 Introduce

Bring in as many of the clothing items shown on the page as you can. See if student know the word for each item of clothing. Write the words on the board. Then go back, pick up each item, and ask students *What's this?* Students answer in **chorus.** You may also want to have students write the words on pieces of paper to attach to the appropriate item of clothing—as a reminder.

2 Practice

1. Ask yourself questions in the following manner. Let students join in whenever they can.
   > **T:** Is this a dress? (Point to a shirt.)
   >   No, it isn't.
   >   Is this a dress? (Point to a dress.)
   >   Yes, it is.
   >   Is this a hat or a dress?
   > **S:** It's a dress. (Write.)

   Continue this way with all the clothing vocabulary.
2. **Pairwork** (see **Before You Begin**) with the substitution exercise at the top of the page. Remind pairs to switch.
3. **Read** (or play the tape for) the questions and answers in the second exercise.
4. **Pairwork** with the same questions and answers. Check pairs.
5. Divide the class in half. Have one half ask the questions in **chorus;** the other half answer. Switch. Listen for correct pronunciation.

3 Follow Up

Ask students if they know the English word for particular articles of clothing worn in *their* country of origin. Using the English translation whenever possible, make a list of these words. Encourage students to practice substituting them into the dialogues on this page.

Culture Capsule. Unit One introduces names of articles of clothing typically worn in the U.S., Canada, and other European countries. As in all countries, what people in the United States wear depends on climate, occupation, age— and the situation. Inhabitants of the northern states wear hats, coats, scarves, gloves, and probably sweaters too, when they go outside in the winter. Businesspeople in big cities wear suits to work, even women. Students all over the world often wear T-shirts and jeans.

1 Introduce

Point and say (stressing the italicized words):

This is my dress (blouse, shirt).
That is your dress (blouse, shirt).

2 Practice

1. Read (or play the tape for) the page. Pick up a student's book. Say and practice in **chorus:**

   This is your book.
   That is my book. (Point.)
2. Repeat with several other students. Write the two sentences on the board. Underline *this* and *that*.
3. Repeat with other familiar words.

3 Follow Up

1. Have students do **Workbook** page 4.
2. Divide the class into groups of three—two students together and a third apart. Have one group work in front of the class with your help while other students listen. Then the groups work simultaneously.

   S1: *This* is his/her . . . . (pointing to an item of clothing worn by Student 2)
   S2: *That* is his/her . . . . (pointing to an item of clothing worn by Student 3)
   S3: *This* is my . . . (point to an item of clothing he/she is wearing)
   That is his/her . . . (pointing to an item of clothing worn by Student 1)

SEVEN/*Unit 1/7*

Role Play

Excuse me. Is your name Miller?

Yes, it is.

Is this your hat?

MILLER

Yes, it is.

Here you are.

Thank you. I forget everything!

You're welcome.

Thanks, I will.

Come again soon.

Data Bank

a cane   a briefcase   a pen

a purse   a coat   a wallet

NEW VOCABULARY | NEW STRUCTURE

1 Introduce

1. **Read** (or play the tape for) the conversation.
2. Model new vocabulary words and have students repeat them in **chorus**. Point to each of the people in the picture and ask, for example, *Is his name Mr. Miller?* Students answer *Yes, it is* or *No, it isn't.*
3. Walk around the classroom asking individual students—sometimes with the correct information and sometimes not:

   T: Excuse me, is your name . . . ?
   S: Yes, it is./No, it isn't.
   T: Is this your . . . ?
   S: Yes, it is./.No, it isn't.

2 Practice

1. **Read** (or play the tape for) the conversation again.
2. Divide the class in half. Have them read the conversation in **chorus.** Have one half play the first character, the other half play the other character. Switch.
3. **Pairwork.** Have students work with the entire conversation. Check intonation and stress as you walk around the room listening, modeling, and praising pairs.
4. **Data Bank.** Model the words and have students repeat them. Verify that students have interpreted them correctly.

3 Follow Up

Role play. Make name tags with made-up names, one for each student, and distribute them to students. Students work in **pairs** to role play using the name on their name tags. Encourage students to stand up and gesture while they role play. They can substitute items of clothing or other objects around the room—Data Bank objects if you have them. Then have students switch parts.

1 Introduce

Note: This activity helps students develop an awareness of conversation probable responses. The page represents a conversation puzzle. (For more about **Say the Right Thing!**, see **Before You Begin** at the front of this book.) Model any new vocabulary words and have students repeat in **chorus**.

2 Practice

1. **Read** the conversations at the top of the page. Point out that there are two separate conversations on the page. Students follow the dotted lines and choose the correct responses.
2. Go back and **read** the first line of the conversation and have students look at the other column and determine the most appropriate response. Continue until the conversation is completed.
3. Divide the class in half. Have one group read the first part in the first conversation in **chorus** while the other half responds with the second part. Switch parts and then repeat with the second conversation.
4. **Pairwork.** Check intonation and stress as you walk around the room listening, modeling, and praising pairs.
5. **On Your Own.** Make up a conversation for the first situation and model it for the students:

   Excuse me, is your name Dan Rogers? Yes, my name is Dan Rogers.
   Is this your wallet? Yes, it *is* my wallet.
   Here you are. Thank you.
   You're welcome. Good-bye.
6. Try the second conversation. Have students play the second part in **chorus.**

   T: Excuse me, is her name Leona?
   C: Yes, it is.
   T: Is this her cane?
   C: Yes, it *is* her cane.
   T: Here's your cane, Leona.
   C: Thanks.
   T: Come again soon
   C: So long.

3 Follow Up

1. **Pairwork.** By now, students should know the conversations well enough to work with their books closed. Have them work with all the conversations on the page. Do not insist that students reproduce them perfectly.
2. **Writing.** Have students write situations about forgetting or losing items. Students exchange and role play the new situations.

Say the Right Thing!

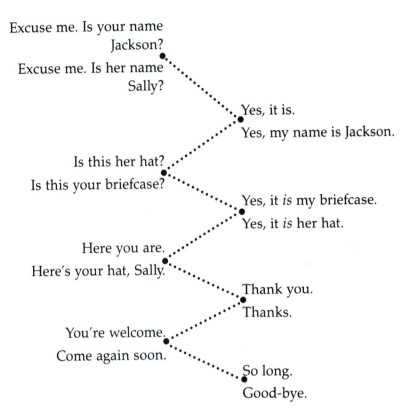

Excuse me. Is your name Jackson?
Excuse me. Is her name Sally?

Yes, it is.
Yes, my name is Jackson.

Is this her hat?
Is this your briefcase?

Yes, it *is* my briefcase.
Yes, it *is* her hat.

Here you are.
Here's your hat, Sally.

Thank you.
Thanks.

You're welcome.
Come again soon.

So long.
Good-bye.

On Your Own

Make conversations with your partner.

1. Your name is Dan Rogers.
   You forget your wallet.

2. Your name is Leona Ching.
   You forget your cane.

3. Your name is Ralph Aceves.
   You forget your pen.

4. Your name is Keiko Tsuyuki.
   You forget your purse.

Pronunciation

I. Hello.
Hello, what's your name?
My name is Ben. What's *your* name?
It's Sally.

II. Is your name Carmen? Yes, it is.
Is his name Peter? Yes, it is.
Is her name Sally or Lucy? It's Sally.

Is your name Mike?
No, it isn't. It's Tom.

III. Lucy, this is my friend, Jack.
Pleased to meet you.
Hello, Lucy. Glad to meet you.

Bye. So long.
See you later.

IV. What's her name?
It's Mary. What's *his* name?
It's Don.

V. Is this your shirt?
No, *that's* my shirt.
Is that *her* scarf?
No, It's *mine.*

NEW VOCABULARY | NEW STRUCTURE

1 Introduce

This is the first of many pronunciation pages provided to supplement the pronunciation guidance and correction that you give regularly as you teach. Only familiar words are used.

Some students may be able to master the rising and falling "tunes" illustrated on this page, but others will place the same stress on conjunctions, articles, and adjectives (*his, her, to*) as they place on content words (*name, wearing, color*). In an English sentence, syllables are not all pronounced at the same rate of speed. Be aware of this and encourage students to imitate correct patterns.

Be sure to insist that students close their lips when producing the *m* sound. Some students tend to leave their lips slightly open.

2 Practice

1. Discuss the arrows that appear above the sentences. They show the general rising and falling tune for the sentence. A statement will usually be a falling tune with an arrow curving downward; a yes-no question will be a rising tune with an arrow curving upward. Alternative questions have the rising tune in the middle.
2. **Read** (or play the tape for) each sentence slowly while students follow silently.
3. **Read** (or play the tape) again with the students repeating in **chorus.** Follow with **T-S, S-S** work.

Predictable Problem. Some students may have difficulty pronouncing the *sh* and *ch* sounds. Students may pronounce *sh* like *ch*. For practice, have students lengthen the *sh* sound (*sh-h-h-h-h*) so it will not become *ch*.

3 Follow Up

Pairwork. Tell students to read alternate sentences to each other. Encourage them to pay attention to the intonation arrows.

1 Introduce

Explain carefully what students are to do: listen and write, on a separate piece of paper, the letter of the picture that best fits the dialogue they hear.

2 Practice

1. **Read** (or play the tape for) the following. Pause long enough between each statement to be sure students have enough time to find and write their answers. (In the taped material, a *pling* indicates the end of each item, and a six-second pause allows the students time to write their answers.) Do not give any repetitions now.

   Number 1
   —David, this is my friend Peter.
   —Glad to meet you Peter.
   —Pleased to meet you David.

   Number 2
   —Hi, Jack.
   —Hello, Don.

   Number 3
   —Good morning, Tom.
   —Good morning, Mary.
   —Is his name John Smith?
   —No, it isn't. It's Ben Wong.

   Number 4
   —Is her name Mary Brown?
   —No, it isn't.
   —Well, what is it?
   —It's Mary Smith.

   Number 5
   —See you later, Mary!
   —Good-bye, Jack!

   Answers
   1. a, 2. c, 3. b, 4. b, 5. c

2. **Read** all five items again, pausing briefly for all students to re-examine their answers.

3 Follow Up

Have students do **Workbook** page 5.

Listen & Understand

| NEW VOCABULARY | NEW STRUCTURE | UNIT ONE 35 |

Fast Track

How are you this morning?

I'm **glad** to hear that.

I am fine.

How are you today?

I am not so well.

I'm **sorry to** hear that.

Now make your own conversations with a partner.

I'm sick!   Great!   Never felt better.   I'm depressed!

12/*Unit 1*/TWELVE

NEW VOCABULARY | NEW STRUCTURE

1 Introduce

In a class of ESL beginners, students have varying amounts of experience with English. Certain students are "false" beginners, that is, they have had some exposure to the language outside the classroom. Some students will have no trouble whatsoever with the material in the unit; others will need practice and/or remediation before moving on to the next unit. (For more about **Fast Track**, see **Before You Begin** at the front of this book.) **Read** (or play the tape for) the conversations. Make sure students understand all the vocabulary.

2 Practice

This material is for students who can handle more practice. Get the faster students started working with the conversations. This will allow *you* to spend time working on the unit with the slower students. Or you could help students who have missed classes catch up on work in the unit.
1. **Read** (or play the tape for) the conversations again.
2. Practice parts of the conversation **T-S, S-S.**
3. **Pairwork.** Have students work with the conversations.
4. Do **pairwork** with the substitution items. Switch.

3 Follow Up

1. Have students do **Workbook** page 6.
2. Have the students who worked with this page act out the conversations for the others. Encourage students to ask other students about words they don't understand. Ask students who worked with the page to write these words on the board and try to explain their meanings.

    You could also come back later and have the students who worked with the material "teach" it to the others. You can follow this plan for all the **Fast Track** activities in the book.

Unit One Test

A. Write the correct response.

1. What's your name? _____

2. Pleased to meet you. _____

3. Good-bye. _____

B. What's the answer?

1. Is this a hat? _____

2. Is this a belt? _____

3. What is it? _____

4. Is this a jacket or a raincoat? _____

C. Fill in the missing words.

1. _____ is her scarf.   2. _____ is her sweater.

D. Circle the correct word or phrase.

1. Excuse me. Is
his
her
your
my
name Smith?   No, my name's Brown.

2. Here you are.
Yes, it is.
Come again, soon.
You're welcome.
Thanks.

Review/Enrich

1. **Picture Box.** Ask students to cut pictures of objects or scenes from magazines or newspapers. Set aside time during the week to discuss the pictures students have collected. Pull out pictures at random and have students describe or name them in English. You can also work with pairs or small groups. Do not insist that students memorize the vocabulary related to these pictures. Continue this throughout the year.

2. **Game 1.** Divide the class into two teams with captains. Write a word on the board, for example, *Tom*. Say the word and indicate that you want a student to tell whether the word on the board is the same word you have just called out. Write *friend*, but say *name*. Continue with various phrases or sentences—*it is* and *it isn't* would be good to use here.

3. **Game 2.** Divide the class into two teams. Write beginning or ending letters of the unit vocabulary words on the board. Show with dash lines the number of missing letters; *fr _ _ _d*. A player must supply the missing letters and pronounce the word to score a point. A more difficult version: Write an entire word with its letters scrambled: *drfeni*. A player must come to the board and write the word correctly to score.

4. **Game 3.** Make small name cards for each student. Pass out the name cards so each student has someone else's name. Students will then walk around the class trying to find the person whose name is on his/her tag. Students will ask *Is his/her name . . . . ?, What's his/her name?, What's your name?* until they find the students named on their cards.

5. **Sentence strips.** Have pairs of students write a sentence from the book on a strip of paper. Students will then cut each word from the sentence strip and scramble the words. Pairs can exchange slips of paper and reconstruct the sentences.

More Communicative Practice

Cut out or have students cut out pictures of famous people from newspapers or magazines. Have students create dialogues involving a famous person, e.g., seeing a famous person at an airport, a famous person forgets his/her jacket in a restaurant, meeting a famous person at a friend's party. Encourage them to express surprise, admiration, excitement, or nervousness—meeting a famous person they might like or dislike

Objectives

Communication

Apologizing
Inquiring/Reporting: *clothing/colors; what people are wearing/doing*
Identifying: *ages*

Grammar

simple statements, yes-no/alternative/information questions
adjectives (color words)
personal pronouns *he, she, it, they*
questions words *what, who*
contractions *that's, who's, he's, she's, they're*

Vocabulary/Expressions

a	he	they
are	jeans	T-shirt
black	or	TV
blue	orange	watching
boots	playing	wearing
brown	purple	white
color	rêd	who
dancing	she	yellow
doing	shoes	Happy birthday!
driving	shorts	Here's a present
favorite	singing	for you.
football	slacks	How old are you today?
glasses	sleeping	Oh no it isn't!
gray	slippers	Sorry!
green	socks	Thank you very much.

Data Bank

1	one	11	eleven
2	two	12	twelve
3	three	13	thirteen
4	four	14	fourteen
5	five	15	fifteen
6	six	16	sixteen
7	seven	17	seventeen
8	eight	18	eighteen
9	nine	19	nineteen
10	ten	20	twenty

Introduce the Unit

Read (or play the tape for) page 13. Let students role play now or later, substituting other clothing names for *hat*.

THIRTEEN/*Unit 2*/13

What's your favorite color? **It's blue.**

brown white red black green

orange purple gray yellow blue

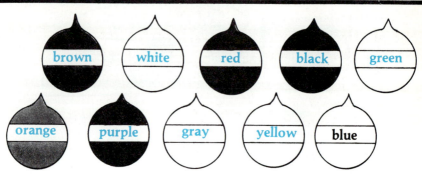

1. What color is his shirt? It's white.

2. What color is her hat? It's gray.

3. What color is his suit? It's black.

4. What color is his bathrobe? It's orange.

5. What color is her skirt? It's green.

6. What color is his jacket? It's yellow.

14/Unit 2/FOURTEEN

NEW VOCABULARY | NEW STRUCTURE

1 Introduce

(Books closed)
1. Describe various students' clothing. Use gestures to point out the article and color.
2. Ask yourself questions in the following manner. Answer appropriately. Let students join in whenever they can:

> **T:** Is this a shirt?
> Yes, it is.
> Is it red?
> No, it isn't.
> Is it blue?
> No, it isn't.
> Is it green?
> Yes, it is.
> Is it red or green?
> **S:** It's green.
> **T:** That's my favorite color. (Translate if necessary.)
> What's your favorite color?
> **S:** It's . . . .

Continue in the same manner with other colors.

2 Practice

1. Have students follow silently as you **read** (or play the tape for) the model question and answer. Work **T-S** with the color substitutions.
2. **Read** (or play the tape for) the questions and answers; **choral work** with the questions, while you read the answers.
3. **Pairwork** with the questions and answers.

3 Follow Up

Have one student come to the front of the room. Allow a minute or so for the class to "study" the student at the front. Have the student leave the room. Then ask the class:

> What color is his/her (dress, skirt, etc.)?

Write the question and answer on the board. Have the student come back and check the answer. You may want to make this game much harder if you have a good group. Ask about everything the student is wearing.

1 Introduce

(Books closed)
1. Quickly review the material on page 14. Go around the room asking individual students:

  T: Is your (jacket, shirt, etc.) blue?
  S: No, my . . . is . . . . /It's . . . .

2. Use gestures to point out articles of clothing that are singular in meaning, but use the plural form, for example, slacks, shorts, jeans, glasses; and clothing worn in pairs, for example, socks, boots, slippers.

  T: What color are his shoes?
  S: His shoes are . . . .
  T: What color are his . . . (jeans, socks, etc.)?
  S: They're . . . . (Prompt, if necessary, and continue with other items of clothing shown on this page.)

3. Write each vocabulary word on the board. Underline the final -s and emphasize the [-s], [-z], or [-iz] sound.

Predictable Problem. Students may be tempted to say *He's wearing* a *shorts* or *She's wearing* a *glasses.* You can explain that articles of clothing consisting of two equal parts which are joined (slacks—two legs, glasses—two eyes) use the plural form.

2 Practice

1. **Read** (or play the tape for) the questions and answers. Students follow silently.
2. **Choral work** with the questions, while you read the answers.
3. **Pairwork.** One student reads the questions, the other reads the answers. Switch roles. Then have pairs practice, type covered, using only the picture cues for prompts.

3 Follow Up

Start asking questions like *What's your favorite color of shoes?* Write *I don't know.* on the board and ask students what it means. Then ask *What's (student's name)'s favorite color of (article of clothing)?* When they answer *I don't know,* tell them to ask the student and then ask again. Continue working **T-S, S-S** in this way.

What color are his shoes?  They're brown.

1. What color are his slacks? They're green.

2. What color are his shorts? They're white.

3. What color are his socks?  They're blue.

4. What color are her boots?  They're black.

5. What color are her slippers?  They're yellow.

6. What color are her jeans?  They're red.

7. What color are her glasses? They're orange.

FIFTEEN/*Unit 2/15*

What's he wearing?  He's wearing
a brown tie.

1. What's he wearing?  He's wearing
a green shirt.

2. What's she wearing? He's wearing
She's wearing
a red blouse.

3. What's she wearing?  She's wearing
a yellow sweater.

What's s(he) wearing?

NEW VOCABULARY | NEW STRUCTURE

1 Introduce

(Books closed)

Note: Do *not* teach the present progressive tense now. *Wearing* is used here because it is logical and useful, and should be considered a vocabulary word, nothing more.

Present *he's/she's wearing* in the following way. Have one student come to the front. Describe him/her.

> **T:** Is . . . wearing a sweater?
> No, s(he) isn't.
> Is s(he) wearing a shirt?
> Yes, s(he)'s wearing a shirt.
> What's s(he) wearing?
> **S:** S(he)'s wearing a shirt.

2 Practice

1. **Read** (or play the tape for) the questions and answers in the usual way, first having the students repeat them in **chorus.**
2. **Pairwork** with the questions and answers.
3. Have students write the answers to the *What's s(he)wearing?* exercise at the bottom of the page. Check students' work. Save these exercises for comparison with written exercises they will do later.

3 Follow Up

1. Have students do **Workbook** page 7.
2. Use the pictures in the book. Ask:
   > **T:** What's s(he)wearing?
   > **S:** S(he)'s wearing . . . .

   Ask another student to write that answer on the board. Continue for each of the articles of clothing pictured.
3. **Choral work** with all the sentences on the board.

1 Introduce

Read (or play the tape for) the questions and answers.

2 Practice

1. **Choral work** with the questions and answers.
2. **Pairwork** as usual.

3 Follow Up

Writing. Assign the *What's s(he)wearing?* exercise at the bottom of the page for written work. Check students' work carefully for proper usage of singular and plural forms.

Progress Check. Use pictures from newspapers or magazines. Make true/false statements about each. If students hear any false statements, they must write the correct descriptive statement.

What's he wearing? He's wearing
white shorts.

1. What's she wearing?  She's wearing
green socks.

2. What's he wearing?  He's wearing
black boots.

3. What's she wearing?  She's wearing
blue slacks.

What's s(he) wearing?

SEVENTEEN/Unit 2/17

Joe is wearing a blue hat.

Sally is wearing a black sweater.

Koko is wearing yellow shoes.

Mike is wearing red slacks.

1. Who's wearing a blue hat?   Joe is.

2. Who's wearing a black sweater?   Sally is.

3. Who's wearing yellow shoes?   Koko is.

4. Who's wearing red slacks?   Mike is.

---

1. Is Mike wearing a red hat?   No, he isn't.

2. Is Mike wearing red slacks?   Yes, he is.

3. Is Sally wearing a red sweater?   No, she isn't.

4. Is Sally wearing a black sweater?   Yes, she is.

5. Is Mike wearing a red hat,
   or red slacks?   He's wearing
   red slacks.

6. Is Koko wearing a yellow blouse,
   or yellow shoes?   She's wearing
   yellow shoes.

7. Is Joe wearing a blue hat,
   or a blue tie?   He's wearing
   a blue hat.

8. Is Sally wearing a black sweater
   or a black skirt?   She's wearing a
   a black sweater.

18/Unit 2/EIGHTEEN

NEW VOCABULARY   NEW STRUCTURE

1 Introduce

(Books closed) Describe a student to the class: *Juanita is wearing a white blouse and a blue skirt. She's wearing brown shoes.* Have students describe various classmates in the same way.

2 Practice

1. Have students **read** the sentences under the pictures silently. Ask them to write a sentence or two describing a classmate. Have them read their sentences to the class.
2. Carry on the following monologue:
   Who's wearing a white shirt? . . .
   (student's name) is.
   Who's wearing black boots? . . .
   (student's name) is.
   Continue and let students join in as soon as they grasp the meaning.
3. **Read** (or play the tape for) the first exercise. Point out that the pictures give the answers to these questions.
4. **Choral work** with the first exercise.
5. **Pairwork** with the same exercise.
6. Then say:
   Is . . . (student's name) wearing a red tie?
   Yes, s(he) is./No, s(he) isn't.
   Repeat with other students' names; allow students to answer in **chorus.**
7. Now say:
   Is . . . (student's name) wearing a red or a blue tie?
   He's wearing a red tie.
   Repeat with several students.
8. Read the second exercise in **chorus.** Again, the pictures give the answers.
9. **Pairwork.** Have pairs ask one another about their classmates after they have practiced the text material.

3 Follow Up

1. Have students do **Workbook** pages 8 and 9.
2. Write some vocabulary words from the first two units on the board. Have students close their eyes while you erase one word. The first person to guess which word was erased gets one point. Continue until all the words have been erased.

1 Introduce

Note: Do *not* teach the present progressive tense now. *Doing, singing, sleeping, etc.* are used here because they are useful, and should be considered vocabulary words, nothing more.

1. Present *he's/she's doing* in the following way. Have a female student come to the front and pretend to be sleeping. Say :
     What's she doing?
     She's sleeping.
     Is she sleeping?
     Yes, she's sleeping.
2. Repeat with a male student. Have him pretend to be driving a car.

2 Practice

1. **Read** (or play the tape) in the usual way, pointing to the pictures in the book.
2. **Choral work** with the questions and answers.
3. **Pairwork.** One student asks the questions and the other answers. Switch roles. Then have pairs practice with the type covered, using only the picture cues for prompts.

3 Follow Up

1. Have students do **Workbook** page 10.
2. Write the names of sports (football, soccer, baseball, basketball, volleyball, etc.) on small pieces of paper or cards—and on the board—and put them face down on your desk. Have a student come and pick one up without telling the others what s(he) picked. The student asks another student *What am I playing?* and the other student guesses. The student who guesses correctly picks up a card and continues in the same manner.

Culture Capsule. The two boys in illustration #4 are shown playing *American* football which is quite different from soccer, commonly called football outside the U.S. and Canada. There are eleven players on each team; all players wear helmets and padding. The football field is 100 yards long; the football (shaped like an oval) may be *thrown* or carried by certain players. A player with the ball may be *tackled*, or brought to the ground forcibly, by members of the opposing team. The team in possession of the ball tries to reach the opponents' end of the field, called the *end zone*. The team is allowed four tries, or *downs*, to make a gain of 10 yards. When a team carries the ball into the end zone, it scores a *touchdown*, which is worth six points.

What's he doing?  He's **singing**.

1. What's she doing?  She's **driving**.

2. What's he doing?  He's **sleeping**.

3. What are they doing?  They're **dancing**.

4. What are they doing?  They're playing American **football**.

5. What are they doing?  They're **watching TV**.

NINETEEN/Unit 2/19

Role Play

NEW VOCABULARY | NEW STRUCTURE

1 Introduce

Encourage students to pretend it is their birthday. Ask *How old are you?* Students can respond with their real ages. (You may have to translate the ages if you have students older than twenty. Write these numbers on the board if necessary.)

2 Practice

1. **Read** (or play the tape for) the conversation. Have students **read** along.
2. Practice parts of the conversation **T-C,T-S.**
3. **Pairwork.** Have students work with the entire conversation. Check intonation and stress as you walk around the room listening, modeling, and praising pairs. Encourage students to stand up and gesture.
4. **Data Bank.** Introduce the numbers 1 to 20. Write them on the board. Model them for the class and have students repeat in **chorus.** If necessary, draw lines or simple objects under each number to help students remember.

3 Follow Up

1. Pretend to give a student a present in a box. Indicate by your actions whether the box is big or small, light or heavy, square or round, or fragile. Have other students guess what is in the box.

   T: Here's a present for you. (giving the box to S1)
   S1:   Thank you. What is it? (taking the box)
   S2:   Is it a . . . (guessing an object)?
   S1:   No, it's not a . . . .
   S3:   Is it a . . . (guessing another object)?
   S1:   No, it's not a . . . . (etc.)
   T: Open it and find out. (to S1)
   S1:   Oh, it's a . . . (anything the student wants to say).
   T: I hope you like it.

2. **Role play.** Students work in **pairs** to practice the conversation. Have them substitute ages and gift items. Volunteers can role play in front of the class.

1 Introduce

Model any new vocabulary words and have students repeat them in **chorus**. Remind students that this page works the same way as the one in Unit 1, that is, once they have chosen from the pair, there are appropriate responses in the following pairs.

2 Practice

1. **Read** the conversations at the top of the page.
2. **Read** different lines from the conversations while you make the appropriate gesture, *Here's a present.* Encourage students to respond with the correct response, *Oh, what is it?* Have them read the correct choice from their book. Then repeat the line and have them try to remember the correct response.
3. Divide the class in half. Have one group read the first part in the first conversation in **chorus** while the other half responds with the second part. Switch parts and then repeat with the second conversation.
4. **Pairwork.** Check intonation and stress as you walk around the room listening, modeling, and praising pairs.
5. **On Your Own.** Make up a conversation for the first situation and model it for the students.
6. Try the second conversation. Have students play the second part in **chorus.**

3 Follow Up

Pairwork. By now, students should know the conversations well enough to work with their books closed. Do not insist that students reproduce the conversations perfectly.

Culture Capsule. Talk about different birthday customs around the world. For example, usually in the United States families and friends get together for a birthday party with hats, decorations, games—and a birthday cake and candles. Ask students if they have heard the birthday song "Happy Birthday to You." Write the words on the board; ask if anyone knows how to sing it. Ask students if they can sing any other birthday songs.

Say the Right Thing!

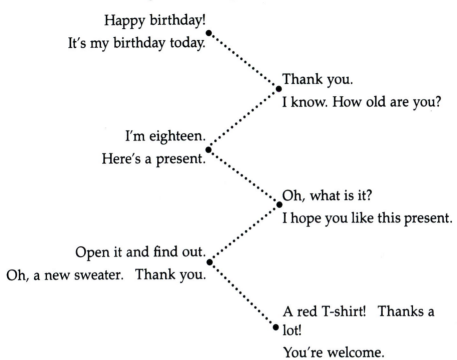

Happy birthday!
It's my birthday today.

Thank you.
I know. How old are you?

I'm eighteen.
Here's a present.

Oh, what is it?
I hope you like this present.

Open it and find out.
Oh, a new sweater. Thank you.

A red T-shirt! Thanks a lot!
You're welcome.

On Your Own

Make conversations with your partner.

1. It's your birthday.
You're twenty.
You get a red hat.

2. It's your sister's birthday.
She's thirteen.
You give her a blue T-shirt.

TWENTY-ONE/Unit 2/21

Read and Enjoy

LAZY JANE

Lazy
lazy
lazy
lazy
lazy
lazy
Jane,
she
wants
a
drink
of
water
so
she
waits
and
waits
and
waits
and
waits
and
waits
for
it
to
rain.

Shel Silverstein

22/Unit 2/TWENTY-TWO

NEW VOCABULARY | NEW STRUCTURE

1 Introduce

1. Students will probably know the difference between prose and poetry in their own language. Ask them to recite short poems. Write *rhythm* and *rhyme* on the board and explain their meaning.
2. Write these pairs of words on the board:
     blue/shoe   dress/yes   shirt/skirt
   Read the words and have students repeat.
3. Then say these pairs of words and ask students to say *yes* if the words rhyme and *no* if they do not:
     you/blue   boot/name   glasses/green   who's/shoes
   Have students repeat the rhyming pairs (*you/blue, who's/shoes*).
4. Check understanding by asking students if they can think of any other pairs of rhyming words. Write them on the board and have students say them.

2 Practice

1. **Read** the poem. Explain anything that students do not understand.
2. Go through the poem **T-C.** The class can read the poem in **chorus.** Ask students to find the words that rhyme. (*Jane/rain*).
3. Ask students which words are repeated in the poem. (*lazy, waits*).
4. Have the class read the poem—starting normally and gradually getting slower and slower as they read the words *waits and waits*, etc. Ask them how seeing and hearing the word *waits* repeated again and again makes them feel.

3 Follow Up

1. Ask students if they enjoy waiting. (No, if it is something bad. Yes, if it is something good.) Ask them how they feel when they are waiting to see the doctor (nervous, afraid), and how they feel when they are waiting for a holiday (happy, excited).
2. Ask them why they think the girl in the illustration, Lazy Jane, wants it to rain. (Because she's thirsty. She wants something to drink. She wants some water.) Finally, ask students if they think the poem is funny and why.
3. **Writing.** Have students work in pairs to brainstorm a poem of their own. It does not have to rhyme, but feel free to supply students with words they want/need if they're attempting rhyme. Encourage pairs to read their poems aloud.

1 Introduce

Explain carefully what students are to do: listen and write, on a separate piece of paper, the letter of the picture that best fits the dialogue, or description.

2 Practice

1. **Read** (or play the tape for) the following. Pause long enough between each statement to be sure students have enough time to find and write their answers. (In the taped material, a pling indicates the end of each item, and a six-second pause allows the students time to write their answers.) Do not give any repetitions now.

Number 1
—Excuse me, is this your hat?
—No, it isn't. That's my hat over there.

Answers
1. c, 2. b, 3. c, 4. a, 5. b

Number 2
—What color is your jacket?
—It's green.
—Is green your favorite color?
—No, it isn't.
—What is your favorite color?
—Blue.

Number 3
Mary's wearing a yellow sweater, a white skirt and brown shoes.

Number 4
Ben's wearing a tie, a shirt, shoes and jeans. His tie is black. His shirt is yellow and his jeans are blue.

Number 5
—Is Tom wearing shorts?
—No, he isn't.
—Is he wearing jeans?
—Yes, he is.
—Is he wearing boots?
—No, he isn't.

2. **Read** all five items again, pausing briefly for all students to re-examine their answers.

3 Follow Up

Have students do **Workbook** page 11.

Listen & Understand

TWENTY-THREE/*Unit* 2/23

Fast Track

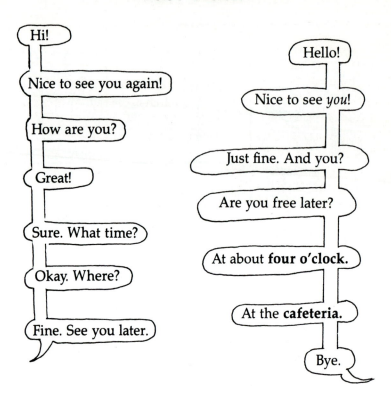

Hi!

Hello!

Nice to see you again!

Nice to see *you*!

How are you?

Just fine. And you?

Great!

Are you free later?

Sure. What time?

At about **four o'clock.**

Okay. Where?

At the **cafeteria.**

Fine. See you later.

Bye.

Now make your own conversations with a partner.

restaurant

office

library

park

| NEW VOCABULARY | NEW STRUCTURE |

1 Introduce

This material extends vocabulary and expressions for greeting, making arrangements, and leave-taking.
1. **Read** (or play the tape for) the entire conversation. Make sure students understand all the vocabulary. Explain that in casual conversation, people often use incomplete sentences to express themselves.
2. Write the following phrases on the board and ask students to expand them into complete sentences:
 Just fine. (I'm just fine.)
 And you? (And how are you?)
 What time? (What time do you want to meet?)
 Where? (Where do you want to meet?)
 See you later. (I'll see you later.)

2 Practice

1. **Read** (or play the tape for) the conversation again.
2. Practice parts of the conversation **T-S, S-S.**
3. **Pairwork.** Have students work with the entire conversation.
4. Do **pairwork** with the substitution items. Switch.

3 Follow Up

1. Have students do **Workbook** page 12.
2. Come back to this page after text page 30 or pages 98–99 to practice expressions of time and the preposition *at.* It will be new for students who do not work with this page in the unit.

A. Match the questions and answers.

_____ 1. What color are his glasses?
_____ 2. What's he wearing?
_____ 3. What color is her sweater?
_____ 4. Is Mike wearing a red hat or red slacks?
_____ 5. What's she wearing?

a. She's wearing a green blouse.
b. It's yellow.
c. Mike is wearing a red hat.
d. They're red.
e. He's wearing blue boots.

B. Circle the correct word.

1. What color is   his jacket?
               are

2. They   is blue.
   It

3. What color is   her shoes?
               are

4. They   are   red.
          is

5. He
   They   are watching TV.
   It

6. How old are you?   He is
                      I am   eleven.
                      You are

C. Write the numbers.

10 _____   7 _____   20 _____

8 _____   11 _____   15 _____

Review/Enrich

1. This is the time for you to work with a small group of students who need extra help. Select the students who require individual attention while the others begin making flashcards. (See Activity 3 below.) Go back to any pages students need to review. Work more quickly than usual, but spend adequate time on each problem.

2. **Pronunciation.** Call out the following words:

blouse	boots	slacks	his	the
jacket	socks	red	glasses	they
shirts	yellow	yes	orange	this
brown	here	tie	jeans	that

   Ask the students to raise their hands when they hear a word ending in -s (for example). Have volunteers write each word on the board.

   Note: The *th* sound does not occur in all languages and is often a difficult one for many students to reproduce easily. Students may pronounce the *th* as a soft *d* or *z* sound. This becomes *dis* or *zis*. You may want to spend a few minutes showing students how to form this sound, but do not insist on perfect pronunciation.

3. **Flashcards.** Have students begin making flashcards for the vocabulary of each unit. The cards can be kept in a box or in the classroom, and various games can be played with them. Pairs or small groups can also use the cards for review. Some students may want to make a set for themselves.

4. **Role playing.** Choose one student to help you "set the scene" for acting out a dialogue.

   > **T:** Excuse me, is this your . . . ?
   > (picking up something from desk or floor)
   > **S:** No, it isn't./Yes, it is. Thank you.
   > (taking it, looking at it, and giving it back)

   Let pairs of students act out the dialogue.

5. **Game.** Divide the class into two teams. The first team picks a color and a team-appointed recorder writes the color name on the board. The second team must name as many common objects usually found in that color as they can within one minute. The recorder writes them on the board. Award ten points if the object is called out by its English name; two if given in the native language. Let teams switch.

6. **Song.** Use the model teaching plan on page 279 to introduce the song "Colors." Words and activities for the song are on page 280.

Objectives

Communication

Inquiring/Reporting/Identifying: *where things/people are; household furniture, rooms; time on the hour/half hour/quarter hour; directions, prices*

Grammar

simple statements, information questions
prepositions *on, under, in front of, behind, at, in*
personal pronoun *we + are*
time structures (*What time is it?, quarter to/past, half past, It's . . . o'clock.*)
question words *where, when*
contractions *where's, I'm, we're, don't*
definite article *the*

Vocabulary/Expressions

				Data Bank
armchair	chair	noon	where	30 thirty
at	children	not	yard	40 forty
bathtub	floor	now	Can you change a dollar?	50 fifty
bed	grandmother	on	Exact fare, please.	60 sixty
bedroom	in	rug	Fares, please.	70 seventy
behind	in front of	sofa	I'm sorry, I don't know.	80 eighty
bus	lamp	table	What time is it?	90 ninety
bus stop	library	the	half past five (five-thirty)	100 hundred
car	living room	under	(two) o'clock.	
cat	midnight	we	quarter past six	
	next	when	quarter to ten	

Introduce the Unit

1. **Read** (or play the tape for) this page once. Point out that the "thought" bubbles show the exact meanings of the sentences.
2. **Choral work** followed by **pairwork.**

3

Where's my jacket?

It's on the sofa.

Where's my raincoat?

It's in the bedroom.

Where are my boots?

They're under the chair.

TWENTY-FIVE/*Unit 3/*25

Where's the tie?
It's on the table.

Where's the hat?
It's on the chair.

Where's the belt?
It's under the chair.

Where's the shirt?
It's under the table.

1. Where's the raincoat?  It's on the chair.

2. Where's the bathrobe?  It's under the table.

3. Where's the scarf? It's on the bed.

4. Where's the sweater?  It's under the sofa.

1 Introduce

1. Show the difference between *a tie* and *the tie* by saying:

What's this?	What's this?
It's a tie.	It's a hat.
The tie is blue.	The hat is brown.

2. Introduce *chair* and *table* by saying:

What's this? (Touch a chair.)	What's this? (Touch a table.)
It's a chair.	It's a table.

3. Put a tie, then a hat on the table and say *The (tie/hat) is on the table.*
4. Place a book on the table and say *Where's the book? The book is on the table.* Continue with other objects. Write *where is* and *where's* on the board. Explain if necessary.

2 Practice

1. **Read** (or play the tape for) the examples at the top of the page; practice in **chorus**. Students should understand the meaning of all the sentences from the pictures.
2. **Read** (or play the tape for) the other four questions and answers; practice in **chorus.**
3. **Pairwork.** Then have pairs practice, type covered, using only picture cues for prompts.

3 Follow Up

Work **T-C** and then **T-S** with these questions and answers about pictures on the page:

       T: Is the tie on the *table* or on the *chair?*
       C: It's on the *chair.*
       T: Is the hat *on* the chair or *under* the chair?
       C: It's *on* the chair.

Have students do **pairwork** with other questions using *or.*

1 Introduce

(Books closed)

1. Draw a house on the board. Write *house*. Then draw a simple floor plan and label the living and bedroom. Indicate the room:

   T: This is a house.

   This is the living room. (Write *living room*.)

   This is the bedroom. (Write *bedroom*.)

   Is this (point) the living room?

   S: Yes, it is./No, it isn't.

   T: Is this the living room or the bedroom?

   S: It's the . . . .

   T: What's this? (Point to the other room.) (etc.)

   Continue with other new vocabulary words: *floor, table,* etc.

2. Draw a stick figure in the living room. Say:

   T: This is Mary. (students repeat)

   Is Mary in the living room or the bedroom?

   Mary is in the living room.

   Where's Mary?

   S: Mary is in the living room. (Repeat with *bedroom*.)

3. Now tell students there is a story about Lucy in the book. Ask the following questions. Make sure students understand they can choose *any* answers they like. Have students write their guesses on a piece of paper. Pretend that you are guessing too, and write your guesses on the board.

   Is her hat on the chair or on the bed? on the table? on the floor?

   Is her scarf on the floor or on the bed? on the chair?

   Are her slippers on the chair or on the rug? on the floor?

   Write students' guesses on the board.

2 Practice

1. **Read** (or play the tape for) the story about Lucy. Have students identify and correct any "wrong" guesses. Read them in **chorus**.
2. Follow with **choral work** and **pairwork** for questions and answers.
3. Have students close their books. Present the second exercise.
4. Follow with **choral** work and **pairwork** as usual.

3 Follow Up

1. Have students do **Workbook** page 13.
2. **Writing.** Students can come back to this page later. Have them cover the type and write a short paragraph about one of the pictures. They do *not* need to include all the information, and may include some not there.

Lucy is in her bedroom.
Her hat is on the chair.
Her blouse is on the table.
Her scarf is on the floor.
Her bathrobe is on the bed.
Her slippers are on the rug.

1. Where's her hat?	It's on the chair.
2. Where's her blouse?	It's on the table.
3. Where's her scarf?	It's on the floor.
4. Where's her bathrobe?	It's on the bed.
5. Where are her slippers?	They're on the rug.

Ben is in the living room.
His shirt is on the sofa.
His tie is on the chair.
His belt is on the table.
His socks are on the lamp.
His shoes are on the rug.

1. What's on the sofa?
2. What's on the chair?
3. What's on the table?
4. What are on the lamp?
5. What are on the rug?

Mr. Jones Mrs. Rivera Mr. King Miss Black

Mr. Jones is in front of Mrs. Rivera.
Mrs. Rivera is in front of Mr. King.
Mr. King is in front of Miss Black.

Miss Black Mr. King Mrs. Rivera Mr. Jones

Mrs. Rivera is behind Mr. Jones.
Mr. King is behind Mrs. Rivera.
Miss Black is behind Mr. King.

Tom		Mary.
Mary	in front of	Bill.
Joe		Sally.
	is	
Lucy		Jack.
Peter	behind	Lucy.
Carmen		Peter.

	Tom?		
Where's	Joe?	He's	in front of...
	Peter?		
	Mary?		
Where's	Lucy?	She's	behind...
	Carmen?		

1 Introduce

1. Have two students come to the front of the class. Place one student in front of the other. Say:

    T: . . . (Joe) is in front of (. . . Mary).
          . . . (Mary) is behind (. . . Joe).
          Is . . . in front of . . . ?
    S: Yes, s(he) is./No, s(he) isn't.
    T: Is . . . behind . . . ?
    S: Yes, s(he) is./No, s(he) isn't.
    T: Is . . . in front of or behind . . . ?
    S: . . . is in front of/behind . . . .
    T: Where is . . . ?
    S: S(he)'s in front of/ behind . . . .

2. Draw six faces on the board. Let students name them and practice the following in **chorus:**

    (Tom) is in front of/behind (Sally).
    (Sally) is behind/in front of (Tom). etc.

3. Seat students in rows and have them practice the above structures using their own names.

2 Practice

1. **Read** (or play the tape for) the text under the first picture, and have students repeat after you in **chorus.** Have students cover the text and complete the sentences using only the pictures for clues.

    Mr Jones is in front of . . . .
    Mrs. Rivera is in front of . . . . (etc.)

2. Work in the same way with the second picture and text.
3. Have students work in **pairs** asking each other about the people pictured in the text.
4. **Pairwork** with the boxes at the bottom of the page.

3 Follow Up

Ask for three or four volunteers to come to the front and stand together in a line. Have another student tell the class where those students are—in front of or behind each other. Now have a student change his/her classmates' positions. Another student will tell where they are then. Repeat several times.

1 Introduction

Place a book on the floor. Carry on the following dialogue:
    T: Is the book on the chair?
    C: No, it isn't. (Write on the board.)
    T: The book is not on the chair. The book is on the floor.
        It *is not* on the chair. (Write on the board.)
        It's not on the chair. (Write on the board.)
        It isn't on the chair. (Write on the board.)
        It's on the floor.
Make sure everyone sees the two ways to contract *it is not*.

2 Practice

1. **Read** (or play the tape for) the exercise and have the class repeat in **chorus**
2. **Pairwork.**
3. Review by having individual students respond with the text on the right covered. Check correct use of prepositions.

3 Follow Up

1. Have students do **Workbook** page 14.
2. **Progress Check.** Let students place classroom items and/or students around the room. Say:
    The book is on the chair.
    The newspaper is under the table.
    The teacher is behind the students.
    The girl is in front of the boy.
    The letter is on the floor.
Students will say or write *yes* or *no*, depending on where the items and/or students are.

1. Is Tom in the car?  No, he's not.
    He's *under* the car!

2. Is the cat on
    the bed?  No, it's not.
    It's on the *table!*

3. Are the children
    in the yard?  No, they're not.
    They're in the *bathtub!*

4. Is Peter in front of
    the chair? No, he's not.
    He's *behind* the chair!

5. Is the girl under
    the sofa? No, she's not.
    She's *on* the sofa!

6. Are you in the car?  No, I'm not.
    I'm in the *bedroom!*

7. Are you under
    the table?  No, we're not.
    We're *on* the table!

8. Is your grandmother
    behind the armchair? No, she's not.
    She's *in* the armchair!

What time is it?

1. It's one o'clock.

2. It's two o'clock.

3. It's three o'clock.

4. It's quarter to four.

5. It's quarter to five.

6. It's quarter past six.

7. It's quarter past seven.

8. It's half past eight.

9. It's half past nine.

10. It's ten-thirty.

11. It's eleven-thirty.

12. It's twelve o'clock. It's noon.

13. It's twelve o'clock. It's midnight.

What time is it now?

1.

2.

3.

1 Introduce

1. Introduce, if necessary, the numbers and words for 1 to 12. Then draw several circles for clocks. Draw the hands (on the hour) in one at a time. Say and write the time under each clock. Practice *It's . . . o'clock* in **chorus.**
2. Point to one of the clocks and ask: *What time is it?* Go through all the clocks again; erase the sentences and repeat using only the clock faces for prompts.
3. Use the same technique to show the half-hour. Say and write: *What time is it now?* Answer yourself the first few times: *It's half past ten.* OR *It's ten-thirty.* Be sure to point out that either way is correct. Continue practicing on the board until students can provide the half hour patterns with no problem.
4. Now show quarter to/past on your clocks. Ask and then prompt students' answers: *What time is it now? it's quarter to/past eleven*, etc. As usual, ask and answer yourself first.
5. Show 12:00, drawing a sun and a moon on the board for *noon* and *mid-night.*

2 Practice

1. **Read** (or play the tape for) the questions and answers.
2. Have students work in **pairs** with the question and answers. Go around checking pairs.

3 Follow Up

1. Have students do **Workbook** page 15.
2. Have students write answers to the question at the bottom of the page.
3. Students who have not already done the **Fast Track** in Unit 2 on page 30 could go back to it now.

Progress Check. Have students draw a large clock on a piece of paper. Explain that they are to draw clock hands indicating any time they like, *quarter past five, quarter to five, five o'clock*, etc. Students will exchange papers and tell the time to the class.

1 Introduce

Read the title, *At the Bus Stop*. Ask the students what a bus stop is. If no one can answer, point to the picture of the bus at the bottom of the page and tell the class that it is a bus. They should be able to translate or explain bus stop with no further prompting.

2 Practice

1. **Read** (or play the tape for) the first dialogue. Let students explain what they think the last two lines mean. Explain, if necessary.
2. **Read** (or play the tape for) the remaining dialogues.
3. **Choral work** with the rest of the page.

Let volunteers take turns acting out this scene. Encourage them to try acting it out without the help of their books.

3 Follow Up

1. Have students do **Workbook** page 16.
2. In a few days, ask various students to act out this scene. Tell students you will periodically check their retention in this manner. They do not have to say exactly what is in the text. They may change times, for example but their dialogue should run along the same line as that in the text.

AT THE BUS STOP

—Excuse me, what time is it?
—It's one o'clock.
—When is the next bus?
—I'm sorry, I don't know.

1.   2.

—Excuse me, what time is it?
—It's half past one.
—When is the next bus?
—I'm sorry, I don't know.

3.

—Excuse me, what time is it?
—It's quarter to two.
—When is the next bus?
—I'm sorry, I don't know.

4.

5.

Role Play

Data Bank

10	ten	40	forty	70	seventy
20	twenty	50	fifty	80	eighty
30	thirty	60	sixty	90	ninety
				100	one hundred

32/Unit 3/THIRTY-TWO

1 Introduce

Ask students where they live or where they work. Write these phrases on the board—*by bus, by train, by car, on a bicycle, on foot*—and ask students how they usually come to class. For the students who take the bus, ask them what number bus they take. Ask other students what number bus they take home or to work.

2 Practice

1. **Read** (or play the tape for) the conversations. Be sure they understand that the passenger walked from one bus to the right bus (number 83).
2. Practice parts of the conversations **T-C,T-S.**
3. **Data Bank.** Introduce the numbers, pointing out that the numbers are listed in "tens." Count from 1 to 100 in groups of tens. Students repeat in **chorus.**
4. Have students work in groups of three—two playing the bus drivers and the other, the passenger. When you think students know the conversations well enough to work without their books, have them role play, substituting bus numbers, fares, and destinations. If students are having difficulty remember-ing, have them write their "lines" on small pieces of paper or cards. Gradually, with practice, they should be able to work without the cues. It is not important that students reproduce the conversations exactly.

3 Follow Up

Students who are progressing quickly can work in groups or three or four to extend the conversations to include a couple of friends or family members going somewhere on a bus or a train. Supply them with any other vocabulary they need to express frustration at being on the wrong bus, for example, or upset because they may be late.

1 Introduce

Remind students that this page works the same way as the ones in Unit 1 and Unit 2. Model any new vocabulary words and have students repeat them in **chorus**. Here, and in future **Role Play** and **Say the Right Thing!** introductions, you could ask one of your more able students to explain or review vocabulary words that other students may find difficult.

2 Practice

1. **Read** the conversations at the top of the page.
2. Check understanding. **Read** lines from the conversations. Encourage students to respond with the correct response from their book. Then repeat the line and have them try to remember the correct response.
3. Divide the class in half. Have one group read the first part in the first conversation in **chorus** while the other half responds with the second part. Switch parts and then repeat with the second conversation.
4. **Pairwork.** Make sure that they are using rising intonation for questions, even ones that look like affirmative sentences, that is , *This isn't the bus for the bank?*
5. **On Your Own.** Work **T-C, T-S** with the first situation.
6. Try the second conversation. Have students play the second part in **chorus.**

3 Follow Up

1. **Pairwork.** By now, students should know the conversations well enough to work with their books closed. Do not insist that students reproduce the conversations perfectly.
2. Encourage students to extend the conversations to reflect their own experiences riding buses.

Culture Capsule. More people drive cars more miles in the United States than anywhere else in the world. Have students discuss how this differs from transportation in their own country. Ask students to list the advantages and disadvantages of different modes of public and private transportation. Talk about the cost of riding buses, trains, and airplanes. Find out if any students have taken rides on more exotic modes of transportation, such as a snowmobile or a Hovercraft. Ask them about their favorite way to travel.

Say the Right Thing!

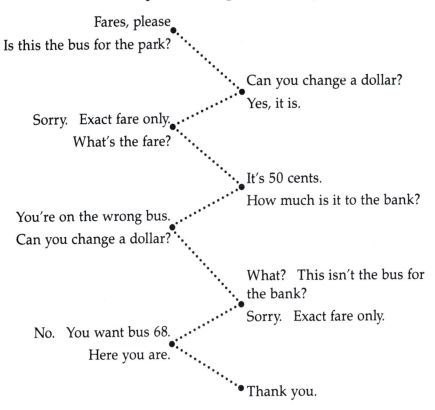

Fares, please

Is this the bus for the park?

Can you change a dollar?

Yes, it is.

Sorry. Exact fare only.

What's the fare?

It's 50 cents.

How much is it to the bank?

You're on the wrong bus.

Can you change a dollar?

What? This isn't the bus for the bank?

Sorry. Exact fare only.

No. You want bus 68.

Here you are.

Thank you.

On Your Own

Make conversations with your partner.

1. You are on the bus.
You ask for the library.
You're on the wrong bus.
You want bus number 33.

2. You are on the bus.
You ask for the post office.
It's 90 cents.
You pay your fare.

Pronunciation

I. Who's wearing a red hat?

Koko is.

Who's wearing shorts?

Peter is.

What color are his shorts?

They're white.

II. What's she wearing?

She's wearing a blue skirt.

What's he wearing?

He's wearing an orange shirt.

What are they doing?

They're watching TV.

III.

hat	lamp	bathrobe	Jack
Sally	children	slacks	that
black	Fred	jacket	glasses

That's my black hat.

Your glasses are under the lamp.

IV. My sweater is black.

Her red hat is on the bed.

My friend is wearing a yellow hat.

The black tie is on the bed.

He's wearing slacks, a bathrobe, and a sweater!

34/*Unit 3*/THIRTY-FOUR

1 Introduce

Write *red* and *glad* on the board. **Read** the following words. Students will raise one hand if the word they hear has the same vowel sound as in *red*; two hands if they hear a word with the same vowel sound as in *glad*.

dancing	yes	Sally	black	jacket	that
glad	hello	hat	red	glasses	bedroom
Ben	well	dress	sweater	slacks	lamp
belt	Jack	bathrobe	yellow	bed	cat

2 Practice

(Books closed for step 1)
1. **Read** (or play the tape for) the words as students follow silently. **Choral work** followed by **T-S, S-S** work.
2. **Pairwork.** One student reads; the other repeats.

Predictable Problem. Students may have difficulty pronouncing the final sounds in the contractions. Model *he's*, *she's,* and *where's* and have students repeat. Then practice pronouncing the words in short sentences with other *z* sounds if possible:
He's wearing slacks. She's wearing shoes.   Where's her scarf?

3 Follow Up

Bring in pictures of familiar vocabulary items. Make sure the items have these vowel sounds: short *a* (*hat, bathrobe, jacket, cat, lamp, glasses, slacks*) and short *e* (*belt, bed, sweater, bedroom, dress*). Mix up the pictures and have students separate them according to the vowel sounds. Write the words in two separate columns on the board as students pronounce them. Have individual students hold up a picture, pronounce the name, and indicate in which column it belongs. Use additional pictures if students know more words.

1 Introduce

Explain carefully what students are to do: listen and write, on a separate piece of paper, the letter of the picture that best fits the dialogue or description.

2 Practice

1. **Read** (or play the tape for) the following:

Number 1
—Where's my tie?
—Is it on the table in the bedroom?
—No, it isn't.
—Is it on the bed?
—No, it isn't.
—Well, is it under the bed?
—Oh, yes! Thank you.

Answers
1. b, 2. a, 3. c, 4. c, 5. a

Number 2
Lucy is in her bedroom. Her hat is on the chair.
Her shoes are under the table. Her skirt is on the bed.

Number 3
Peter is in the living room. He is on the rug.
His jacket is on the chair and his shoes are under the sofa.

Number 4
—Excuse me, when is the next bus?
—At quarter to eleven.
—What time is it now?
—It's quarter past ten.

Number 5
—Where's Mrs. Rivera?
—She's behind Mr. Jones.
—Mr. Jones? Where is he?
—He's behind Mr. Smith.

2. **Read** all five items again, pausing briefly for all students to re-examine their answers.

3 Follow Up

Have students do **Workbook** page 17.

Listen & Understand

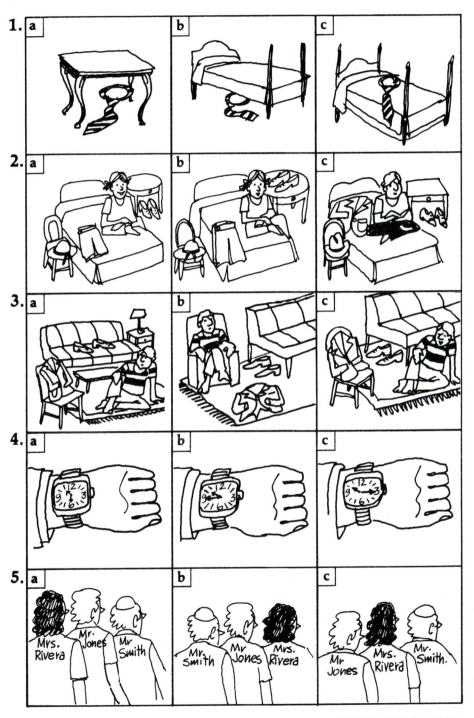

Fast Track

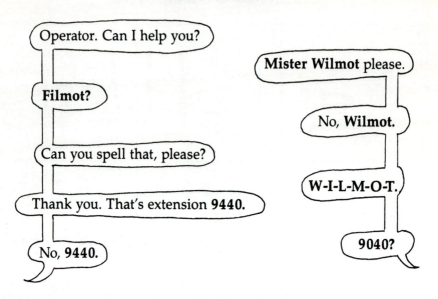

Operator. Can I help you?

Mister Wilmot please.

Filmot?

No, **Wilmot.**

Can you spell that, please?

W-I-L-M-O-T.

Thank you. That's extension **9440.**

9040?

No, **9440.**

A	B	C	D	E	F	G	H	I	J	K	L	M
N	O	P	Q	R	S	T	U	V	W	X	Y	Z

Now make your own conversations with a partner.

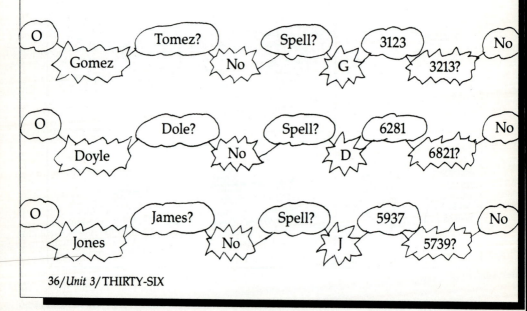

O — Gomez — Tomez? — No — Spell? — G — 3123 — 3213? — No

O — Doyle — Dole? — No — Spell? — D — 6281 — 6821? — No

O — Jones — James? — No — Spell? — J — 5937 — 5739? — No

1 Introduce

Read (or play the tape for) the entire conversation. There is little new vocabulary here, but students get a lot of practice with letters and numbers. These conversations are meant to be humorous, so you can encourage students to exaggerate while practicing them. Working in this way may also help students feel more relaxed about the possibility of misunderstanding someone else or being misunderstood themselves.

2 Practice

1. **Read** (or play the tape for) the conversation again.
2. Practice parts of the conversation **T-S, S-S.**
3. **Pairwork.** Have students work with the entire conversation.
4. Do **pairwork** with the substitution items. Switch.

3 Follow Up

1. Have students do **Workbook** page 18.
2. Have students work in **pairs.** One person pronounces the name of a person or place and the other tries to write it down. If s(he) has trouble, s(he) can ask the first person to spell the name. Repeat for several names, and then switch roles. Students can use English names or names from their own language if it uses the English alphabet.

A. Circle the correct word.

       am
1. Where is my boots?
       are

       are
2. Where am my jacket?
       is

       am
3. Where is you?
       are

       am
4. Where is they?
       are

B. Write the correct responses.

Where's the ball?

1. _____   2. _____

Where's Mary?

3. _____   4. _____

C. What time is it?

1. _____

2. _____

3. _____

Review/Enrich

1. Tell students to close their eyes and listen carefully. If they hear *on* in a sentence, they are to put their hands on their desks. If they hear *under*, they are to put their hands under their desks or chairs.

    The tie is on the table.   The jacket is under the table.
    The book is under the chair.   It's on the chair.
    It's under the table.

2. Use page 26 and practice the following:

    T: Is the hat on the chair/on the table/under the chair/table?
    C: Yes, it is./No, it isn't.
    T: Is the hat *under* the chair or *on* the chair?
    C: It's . . . the chair.
    T: Where's the belt?
    C: It's on/under the . . .

3. Review prepositions by having students stand or sit in various places in the class. When a volunteer has placed him/herself in X place, another student describes where s(he) is. If the student is right, s(he) takes the next turn.

4. Ask students to help you make a list of words on the board that are names of something. If you wish, you may teach the term *noun*. Explain that nouns name people or things. Once you have listed 10 or 12 words, ask students to make sentences using the words, orally or in writing.

More Communicative Practice

Have students work in groups of three to role play the following situation. You come home to find someone has broken into your house/apartment/room and the place is a mess. You phone the police to report the break-in. You talk to the police and another family member checks around and answers the questions. The dialogue could sound like this:

S1:	Is your bathrobe in the bedroom?
S2:	(to S1) I don't know.
	(to S3) Is my bathrobe in the bedroom?
S3:	Yes, it's in the bedroom.
S1:	Is it on the floor?
S2:	(to S3) Is it on the floor?
S3:	Yes, it's on the floor.
S1:	Is it under the bed?
S2:	(to S3) Is it under the bed?
S3:	No, it's not. It's behind the chair? (etc.)

Objectives

Communication
Reporting: *describing people*
Inquiring/Reporting: *identifying people by what they are wearing; food, likes/ dislikes; prices*

Grammar
verb *to be* + predicate adjective
pronunciation of [-s], [-z], [-iz] sounds
question words *how old, how much*

Vocabulary/Expressions

				Data Bank
and	egg(s)	man	tall	calculator
apple(s)	eyes	new	that	magazine
beans	girl	nuts	there	newspaper
blond(e)	girlfriend	oranges	thin	notebook
book	grapes	over there	very	
boy	guy	owner	woman	
boyfriend	hair	pants		
buying	handsome	peach(s)	Anything else?	
candy bar(s)	how much	pear(s)	Can I help you?	
carrot(s)	how old	please	Here's your change.	
cent(s)	last (name)	pretty	How much is that?	
chubby	like	sandwich(es)	Is that all?	
do	look	short	Nice to meet you.	
dollar(s)	look at	store	What's (s)he like?	

Introduce the Unit

Students will spend considerable time describing themselves and others with new and old vocabulary. For the first time, they are asked to use a model dialogue and substitute words (see text page 38). This is a valuable technique for encouraging students to use and extend the language in context.

Read (or play the tape for) the short dialogues. Students already know *that* used as a pronoun—*Oh, that's Joe. That* is also used as an adjective in this dialogue—*Who's that guy?*

Note: The word *guy* is slang for boy or man. It should be used in informal conversation only. Students may know the expression *you guys*, which is a very informal expression used by young people to refer to a group of friends.

4

—Who's that guy over there?
—Where?
—There — the guy in the green pants.
—Oh, that's Joe.

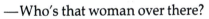

—Who's that woman over there?
—Who? Where?
—There — the woman in the blue dress.
—Oh, that's Jane.

THIRTY-SEVEN/*Unit 4/37*

1. Who's this?
   How old is she?
   What color is her hair?
   Is she thin or chubby?
   And what color are her eyes?

Lucy

19

   It's Lucy.
   She's nineteen.
   It's black.
   She's chubby.
   They're black.

13

2. Who's this?
   How old is he?
   What color is his hair?
   Is he tall or short?
   And what color are his eyes?

Daniel

   It's Daniel.
   He's thirteen.
   It's blond.
   He's short.
   They're green.

14

Bill

3. Who's this?
   How old is **he**?
   What color is **his** hair?
   What color are **his** eyes?
   Is **he** thin or chubby?
   Is he tall or short?

   It's **Bill**.
   He's fourteen.
   It's **red.**
   They're **blue.**
   He's chubby.
   He's tall.

Elena

16

Joe

15

1 Introduce

1. Ask a student to come to the front of the class. Say and write:
   > This is . . . (student's name).
   > S(he)'s . . . (age of student).
   > His/her hair is . . . (color).
   > His/her eyes are . . . (color).
2. Now ask:
   > Who's this?
   > How old is s(he)?
   > What color is his/her hair?
   > What color are his/her eyes?
3. Bring another student to the front and repeat the procedure. Be sure to include several male and female students for *his/her* practice.

2 Practice

1. **Read** (or play the tape for) the page.
2. Work **T-C, T-S** with the first two dialogues. Explain any new words.
3. **Pairwork**.
4. **Choral work** with the questions and answers in #2 above. Point out the **bold face** type in this dialogue. Explain that these are key words the students will have to change to describe Joe and Elena, the two characters at the bottom of the page. Make sure everybody understands how the substitutions work, as this technique will be used often from now on.
5. Work **T-C, T-S** with the same exercise. You will ask the questions; students will answer in **chorus** and individually.

3 Follow up

Writing. Have students write descriptions of Joe and Elena.

1 Introduce

1. Draw two faces on the board and ask *What's his/her name?* Students can give any names. Now say and write on the board:

   This is . . . (Tom).
   This is . . . (Mary).
   Mary is his girlfriend. (Indicate.)
   Tom is her boyfriend. (Indicate.)
   Tom is handsome. (Explain.)
   Mary is beautiful. (Explain.)

2. Practice the above sentences in **chorus.** Continue with the following and explain any new words.

   This is Tom.
   His last name is King.
   What's he like? (Be sure students understand that here this means *What does he look like?*)
   He's very tall and thin.
   He's seventeen.

3. Practice in **chorus** from the board.

Note: In English you usually say the given name first and the family name last: thus, the terms *first name* and *last name*.

2 Practice

1. **Read** (or play the tape for) the first dialogue while students follow silently. Explain the new vocabulary.
2. Work **T-C** with the two picture cue substitutions. then do **pairwork.**
3. Work **T-C** with the second and third dialogues.

3 Follow Up

1. Have students do **Workbook** page 19.
2. Students can take turns describing themselves and each other. Encourage them to use as many of the new vocabulary words as possible.

Culture Capsule. It is often considered impolite in English-speaking cultures to ask an older adult's age. For example, it would not be appropriate to ask a friend his/her parents' ages in a social situation. The same rule applies to height and weight. Of course, if you were filling out an official form that required age, height, and weight, you would ask—even an older person.

—Look at that woman over there.
—Where?
—There—the woman
  in the red dress.
—Oh, that's Elena.
—What's her last name?
—It's Rivera.

1. man /Sam/Chin

2. boy /Tim/Novak

—Look, this is Ted.
—Is he your new boyfriend?
—Yes, he is.
—What's he like?
—Well, he's thin. His hair is
  red, and his eyes are green.
  He's very tall and handsome.
  And he's twenty-four.

—Look, this is Rita.
—Is she your new girlfriend?
—Yes, she is.
—What's she like?
—Well, she's short and chubby.
  Her hair is blonde, and her
  eyes are blue. She's thirty-
  one and very pretty!

Who's this?
What's **his** last name?
How old is **he**?
Is **he** tall or short?
Is **he** chubby or thin?
What color is **his** hair?
What's **he** wearing?

It's **Frank.**
It's **Mann.**
He's **twenty.**
He's **short.**
He's **thin.**
It's **brown.**
He's wearing
a white shirt,
a gray tie,
a blue jacket,
brown slacks and
black shoes.

Frank Mann

1. Joe Nunez   2. Susie Wong   3. Tim Grubb   4. Pat Pratt

40/Unit 4/FORTY

1 Introduce

Now students should be able to handle a fairly long dialogue with a number of substitution items. You may wish to ask leading questions about Frank Mann and write students' guesses on the board.

2 Practice

1. **Read** (or play the tape for) the dialogue as usual. Go through it again asking questions about Frank Mann with the class answering in **chorus**. Ask two students to use the dialogue to describe one of the characters at the bottom of the page. Students must substitute appropriate nouns, pronouns, and adjectives in the model dialogue in order to describe the four characters shown.
2. **Pairwork.** Go around the room checking pairs.

3 Follow Up

1. Have students do **Workbook** pages 20 and 21.
2. **Writing.** Have students write a description for one or two of the characters shown at the bottom of the page.

Progress Check. At first students may have difficulty pronouncing the *-teen* numbers. The stress goes on the *-teen* and it has a long *e* sound. Listen carefully to make sure students are pronouncing these numbers correctly. It is especially important so that they will be prepared for discriminating between numbers like *thirteen* and *thirty*.

1 Introduce

1. Place a book on your desk and say *What's this? It's a book.* Put another book there and (stressing the final [-s]) say *Now, two books.* Continue adding books and stressing the final [-s]. Count forward and backward in **chorus.** Write *one book, two books* on the board.
2. Repeat above exercise with pencils, stressing the final [-z] sound.
3. Write the following model question and answer on the board:
   T: Do you like apples?
   S: Yes./No. (Repeat with all food vocabulary.)

2 Practice

1. **Read** (or play the tape) in the usual way. Ask students to read questions 7, 8, and 9 aloud. Write *oranges, peaches, sandwiches*; circle the *-s* and *-es* endings, pointing out that only the -es form adds another syllable.
2. Work **T-C, T-S, S-T, S-S** in the usual way with all the questions and answers.

3 Follow Up

Write headings [-s], [-z], and [-iz] on the board. Tell students to listen carefully as you say the following words. Have various students write each word under the correct heading on the board.

glasses [-iz]	peaches [-iz]	skirts [-s]
hats [-s]	tables [-z]	shoes [-z]
socks [-s]	jackets [-s]	sandwiches [-iz]

Yes.

Do you like apples? No.

1. Do you like carrots?

2. Do you like nuts?

3. Do you like grapes?

4. Do you like pears?

5. Do you like candy bars?

6. Do you like beans?

7. Do you like oranges?

8. Do you like peaches?

9. Do you like sandwiches?

What's she buying?   She's buying eggs.

What's she buying?   She's buying carrots.

What's she buying?   She's buying pears.

What's she buying now?

1.

2.

3.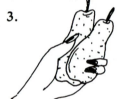

4.

5.

6.

7.

8.

9.

*42/Unit 4/*FORTY-TWO

1 Introduce

Read (or play the tape for) the questions and answers in the box. Explain *buying* if necessary and read again in **chorus**.

2 Practice

1. Work **T-C, T-S** with the question and nine picture cues at the bottom of the page. Note that all the plural or mass nouns have no article.
2. **Pairwork.**

3 Follow Up

Have students do **Workbook** page 22.

Predictable Problem. The final *-ng* is difficult for some students to pronounce correctly. Students may try to say *-n* instead of *-ng*.

Drill words such as *morning, long, wearing, buying, living, sitting, eating, drinking* along with words with a final *-n: an, brown, green, noon, on, when, ten, man, thin.* You may want to have students listen for the final sounds; raise one hand when they hear final *-n,* and two hands when they hear *-ng*.

1 Introduce

The students know most of the words and phrases in this dialogue. Use the technique we call **Build Up the Board,** which is similar to the guessing game, to introduce this page. Proceed in the following manner:

> **T:** Where's Sally?
> She's in the store. (Explain if necessary and write on the board.)
> What's she doing?
> **S:** She's buying . . . . (Write on the board.)
> **T.** Juan is in the store.
> What's he doing?
> **S:** He's buying . . . . (Write on the board.)

Set up a store situation. You role play the store keeper and ask a student to play the customer. Write the dialogue on the board as you go along. Work in **chorus.**

> **T:** Hello, Sally.
> **S:** Hello.
> **T:** Can I help you? (Explain if necessary.)
> **S:** Yes, (eight candy bars, five oranges, etc.). (Prompt if necessary.)
> **T:** Here you are. Anything else?
> **S:** Yes, ... /No.
> How much is that? (Prompt if necessary.)
> **T:** That's . . . dollars, please.
> **S:** Thanks.
> **T:** Thank you.

Call another student up to the front and repeat with a similar exchange. Then have students do **pairwork** with the dialogue. Erase parts of the dialogue as they work, so they will rely on their memories rather than reading from the board.

2 Practice

1. Ask students to listen for one fact, that is, how much the items cost or what was purchased. **Read** (or play the tape for) the dialogue.
2. Let students work in groups of three. Groups should role play at the front. They may substitute foods and how much they cost.

3 Follow Up

Discuss students' food likes and dislikes. Have them ask each other *Do you like pears?* or *What is your favorite food?* You may want to discuss local foods. Write *with* on the board. Tell them a food that you like to eat with another food, for example, *I like yogurt with fruit.* Ask what they like to eat with their favorite foods.

IN THE STORE

Dick is in the store.
Carol is in the store.
Mrs. Hill is in the store.
She is the owner.

MRS. HILL: Hello, Dick.

DICK: Hello, Mrs. Hill.

This is my friend, Carol.

MRS. HILL: Hello, Carol.

Pleased to meet you.

CAROL: Hello, Mrs. Hill.

Nice to meet *you*.

MRS. HILL: Can I help you?

DICK: Eight candy bars, please.

MRS. HILL: Here you are.

Anything else?

CAROL: Yes, six

sandwiches, please.

MRS. HILL: Is that all?

DICK: Yes, thanks,

How much is that?

MRS. HILL: That's four dollars, please.

CAROL: Here you are.

Thank you.

FORTY-THREE/*Unit 4/43*

Role Play

Can I help you?

How much is this pen?

It's fifty cents.

And how much is this book?

It's a dollar.

Here's two dollars.

Thank you. And here's your change.

Thank you. Bye.

Data Bank

a notebook

a newspaper

a magazine

a calculator

1 Introduce

1. Read (or play the tape for) the conversation.
2. Write the word *stationery* on the board and explain. Ask students for stationery items they know in English and make a list on the board. (Save the list for substitution practice below.)

2 Practice

1. **Read** (or play the tape for) the conversation again.
2. Divide the class in half. Have them read the conversation in **chorus.** Have one half play the first character, the other half play the other character. Switch.
3. **Pairwork.** Have students work with the entire conversation. Encourage students to stand up and gesture while they role play.
4. **Data Bank.** Introduce words from the Data Bank, which students can substitute in the conversations. They can also substitute items still listed on the board.

3 Follow Up

If some students are working easily with the material, have them extend the conversation to other situations, for example, a bakery. Encourage them to create real situations with real prices.

1 Introduce

1. Students may need to review larger numbers, especially the difficult ones. Have several students write the numbers from 20 to 100 on the board. Point to several numbers and have students say them in **chorus.** Then point to several numbers and have students write the number in words. Write the answers on the board and have students check their own work.
2. Introduce the expression *How about . . . ?* in the following way:

   T: What's your name?
   S: It's . . . .
   T: How about you? (to another student)
   S: My name's . . . .
   T: What's your favorite fruit?
   S: . . .
   T: How about you? (etc.)

2 Practice

1. **Read** the conversations. If possible, ask for students' help in following the correct sequence. Pretend, for example, that you are having trouble figuring out the next line. Elicit the correct line from the class.
2. Divide the class in half. Have one group read the first part in the first conversation in **chorus** while the other half responds with the second part. Switch parts and then repeat with the second conversation.
3. **Pairwork.**
3. **On Your Own.** Have students role play the situations.

3 Follow Up

Encourage students to extend the conversation to reflect their own shopping experiences. Help them with vocabulary they might need to express surprise, for example, if the prices are especially low or high!

Say the Right Thing!

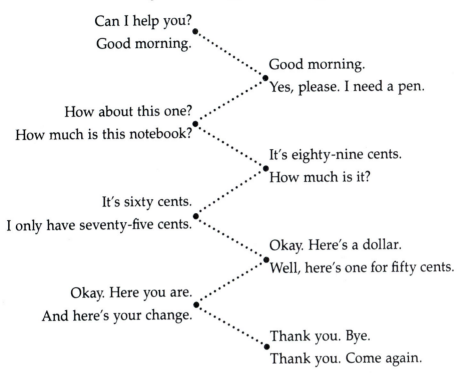

Can I help you?
Good morning.

Good morning.
Yes, please. I need a pen.

How about this one?
How much is this notebook?

It's eighty-nine cents.
How much is it?

It's sixty cents.
I only have seventy-five cents.

Okay. Here's a dollar.
Well, here's one for fifty cents.

Okay. Here you are.
And here's your change.

Thank you. Bye.
Thank you. Come again.

On Your Own

Make conversations with your partner.

You need a pen.
You ask how much it is.
It's two dollars.
You have a five dollar bill.

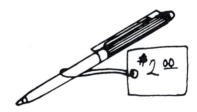

Read and Enjoy

I AM RUNNING IN A CIRCLE

I am running in a circle
and my feet are getting sore,
and my head is
spinning
spinning
as it's never spun before,
I am
dizzy
dizzy
dizzy.
Oh! I cannot bear much more,
I am trapped in a
revolving
. . . volving
. . . volving
. . . volving door!

Jack Prelutsky

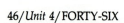

1 Introduce

Read (or play the tape for) the poem. Explain anything that students do not understand. Ask them which words are repeated in the poem (*spinning, dizzy, revolving*). Explain that these words all relate to the action of turning around in a circle. Ask them how it makes them feel when they hear these words again and again (feel dizzy).

2 Practice

1. Go through the poem **T-C.** The class can read the poem in **chorus.** Ask students to find the words that rhyme. (*sore/before/more/door*).
2. **Read** the poem line by line as you clap out the rhythm. Students repeat. Ask students to tell you how many stresses each "line" gets in the poem (4).
3. Practice pronouncing the words in the poem that end in *-ing* (*spinning, revolving*).

3 Follow Up

Have students each memorize one or more lines of the poem. Then have them recite the poem in "relay." If some students are having trouble remembering, they can write down their line(s) . If students are missing the rhythm, have the class clap the rhythm as they recite.

1 Introduce

Explain carefully what students are to do: listen and write, on a separate piece of paper, the letter of the picture that best fits the dialogue or description.

2 Practice

1. **Read** (or play the tape for) the following:

Number 1
—Hello, Lucy.
—Hello, Don.
—Who's that boy over there?
—Who?
—The boy in the blue shirt.
—Oh, that's John.

Answers
1. c, 2. b, 3. a, 4. a, 5. b

Number 2
—Can I help you?
—Yes, these eggs, please.
—Is that all?
—Yes, thank you.

Number 3
—Do you like sandwiches?
—Yes, I do.
—Are you buying grapes or oranges now?
—No, I'm buying sandwiches.

Number 4
—Pat's wearing a blue hat, a white scarf and a purple blouse.

Number 5
—That's my girlfriend over there.
—The girl in the white dress?
—No, the girl in the blue jeans and white sweater.
—Ah, yes!

2. **Read** all five items again, pausing briefly for all students to re-examine their answers.

3 Follow Up

Have students do **Workbook** page 23.

Listen & Understand

Fast Track

—**Mainframe Computers.**
— Good morning. My name is **Gail Simon.**
— Good morning. What can I do for you?
— I'm interested in the **computer operator**
  job advertised in today's paper.
— Your name again, please?
—**Simon. Gail Simon.**
— And your address, **Ms. Simon**?
—**495 Fremont Avenue,**
  Houston, Texas 77059.
— Fine. I'll send you an
  application. Thank you
  for calling.
— Thank you.

Now make your own conversations with a partner.

Charles Snow of 123 Chestnut
Road, Buffalo New York 14224 is
interested in a job as a receptionist at
the Hilltop Hotel.

Janine Rodriguez of 783 New Haven
Street, Santa Rosa, California 95043 is
interested in a job as a secretary
at Sunshine Travel.

Dennis Chang of 69 Bank Street,
Chicago, Illinois 60646 is interested
in a job as an electrician at Munroe's
Electric Shop.

1 Introduce

1. **Read** (or play the tape for) the entire conversation.
2. Write *Mr., Mrs., Miss, Ms.* (pronounced *Miz*) on the board. Point to each term of address and model its pronunciation. Then point to each and have students pronounce it in **chorus.**
3. There are various verb forms here that students have not seen: *interested, advertised, 'll (will) send, calling.* Explain if necessary, but do not spend a lot of time analyzing the forms.

2 Practice

1. **Read** (or play the tape for) the conversation again.
2. Practice parts of the conversation **T-S, S-S.**
3. **Pairwork.** Have students work with the entire conversation.
4. Do **pairwork** with the substitution items. These substitutions are quite difficult, and students will start out using their books. So they can role play the conversations more naturally, have them write the information on small pieces of paper or cards.

3 Follow Up

1. Have students do **Workbook** page 24.
2. One of the most difficult challenges faced by ESL students is using the telephone. Have students role play the various conversations using their own names. If possible, have the pairs sit back to back as they practice, gesture picking up the telephone, etc.

Culture Capsule. Here students are introduced to more formal greetings. Explain that older boys and men are usually called *Mr.*; girls and unmarried women are addressed as *Miss*; married women are called *Mrs.* Explain that *Ms.* is a relatively new form of address for older girls and women, married or unmarried. Since this is a business situation and the people do not know each other, they use *Ms.* Although people in the United States are generally more informal than the British, for example, advise students to listen for how people are addressing each other. When in doubt, it is usually safer to be more formal.

A. Write the correct questions.

1. _____   It's Lucy.

2. _____   She's nineteen.

3. _____   It's black.

4. _____   She's chubby.

5. _____   They're blue.

B. Write the correct questions.

1. _____   He's short.

2. _____   He's wearing a black jacket.

3. _____   It's Mann, Tom Mann.

C. Do you like . . . ?

1. _____   Yes, I do.

2. _____   No, I don't.

D. Complete the conversation.

1. _____ ?   Yes, eight candy bars, please.

2. _____ .   Thank you.

3. _____ ?   Yes, six apples, please.

4. _____ .   Yes, thanks.

That's six dollars, please.

Review/Enrich

1. Introduce and describe a student with the following:
   This is . . . .
   His hair is . . . (black).
   His eyes are . . . (blue).
   He is . . . (20) years old.
   He is tall. (Show with a gesture.)
   Describe (and let students describe) one or two other students using other adjectives. As new adjectives are mentioned, write them on the board.

2. Now ask alternative questions:
   T: Is his hair black or brown?
   S: It's . . . .
   T: His eyes? Are his eyes green or brown?
   S: (Brown.)
   T: Is he short or tall?
   S: (Tall.)

3. Have students play "police officer" by making a wanted poster that describes one of their classmates. have individual students read their descriptions. The rest of the class must listen carefully and "hunt down" the wanted person.

4. An *adjective* describes, limits, or restricts a noun or pronoun—*She is wearing **black** shoes./Sam is a **tall** man.* You can extend student awareness by listing adjectives with their help. Divide the class into two teams. A student from Team A calls out a sentence (leaving out the adjective):
   Sam is a . . . man.
   She's wearing a . . . skirt.
   Elena is a . . . girl. (etc.)
   Students from Team B must supply a reasonable adjective to complete the sentence. Switch roles.

5. **Song.** Use the model teaching plan on page 279 to introduce the song "Give My Regards to Broadway." Words and activities for the song are on page 281.

More Communicative Practice

Have students write a letter to a new pen pal. In the letter they will describe themselves and some of their likes and dislikes. Show students how to open the letter with *Dear . . . ,* and how to close with *Yours truly,* or *Yours sincerely,* followed by their name.

Objectives

Communication
Inquiring/Reporting: *what people are doing; food/drinks; likes/dislikes*

Grammar
articles *a/an*
plural nouns (count/mass)
present progressive verb forms
pronunciation of [-s] [-z] [-iz] sounds
question words *how many*

Vocabulary/Expressions

an	drinking	milk
banana(s)	eating	need
bread	fish	radio(s)
butter	guitar(s)	reading
cheese	how many	record(s)
chicken	ice cream	room
coffee	lemonade	sitting
comic book	letter	spoon
dear	meat	tea
dog		water

Data Bank

bread	pepper
fork	pizza
fruit	salad
glass	salt
knife	spaghetti
napkin	sugar

Introduce the Unit

Pay special attention to the present progressive tense, and do not worry if the students do not learn *all* the vocabulary perfectly. Students can study independently later to pick up any lexical items they have not fully learned.

Read (or play the tape for) the opening dialogue. Point out that the "thought" bubbles show the exact meanings of the sentences.

5

—Hi, dear.
What's Peter doing?
—He's drinking tea
in the living room.

—What's Mary doing?
—She's buying eggs at the store.

—And the dog?
—He's eating your newspaper.

My newspaper!

What's he eating?

1. He's eating a pear.

2. He's eating a banana.

3. He's eating a candy bar.

4. He's eating an apple.

5. He's eating an egg.

6. He's eating an orange.

What's he eating now?

1.

2.

3.

4.

5.

6.

1 Introduce

Draw an apple on the board. Ask yourself questions:

T: Is this a pear?
No, it isn't.
Is this a banana?
No, it isn't.
Is this an apple? (Write *an apple*.)
Yes, It is.
Is this a pear or an apple?

S: An apple.

T: What's this?

S: It's an apple.

Pretend to give the apple to the student. Indicate that s(he) should pretend to eat it. Say *S(he)'s eating an apple.*

2 Practice

1. **Read** the six statements in the box in **chorus.** Point out the articles *a* and *an.* We use *a* before nouns beginning with consonant sounds; *an* before nouns beginning with vowel sounds.
2. Go on to the second exercise and *What's he eating now?* Work **T-C, T-S** with the picture cues.
3. **Pairwork.**

3 Follow Up

Ask students to give the man at the bottom of the page a name, let's say Ronald. Point to the pictures in the book and work **T-C, T-S** with alternative questions in the following manner:

T: Number 1. Is Ronald eating an apple or an egg?
S: He's eating an egg.
T: Number 2. Is Ronald eating an apple or apples?
S: He's eating an apple.
T: Number 3. Is Ronald sitting in a chair or eating a pear?
S: He's eating a pear.

Continue with yes-no questions and information questions about 1, 2, and 3. Then have students write questions and answers for the last three pictures.

1 Introduce

Review *Do you like . . . ?* and talk about the food items on this page by asking *Do you like pears?* and so on. Work **T-C, T-S, S-S** with the pictures at the bottom of the page.

2 Practice

1. **Read** (or play the tape for) the three sentences at the top of the page. Point out again:

    a banana (*a* before a consonant sound)
    an apple (*an* before a vowel sound)

2. Draw one banana on the board and write *a banana.* Draw two bananas; write *bananas.* Repeat with *an apple, apples*; *an egg, eggs.*
3. Go on to the second exercise and ask *What's she buying?* Work **T-C, T-S,** with all nine pictures.
4. **Pairwork.**
5. Work **T-C** for a final check on vocabulary and use of the articles *a* and *an.*

3 Follow Up

Write the following words on small pieces of paper. Fold up the papers and put them in a box, hat, etc. Students will take turns picking a word and using it in a sentence. You may have students work in **pairs** and make up a question and an answer for each word drawn.

apples	eating	an
buying	drinking	a
she's	he's	lemonade

She's buying a banana.

She's buying an apple.

She's buying eggs.

What's she buying?

1.	2.	3.
4.	5.	6.
7.	8.	9.

What's he drinking?  He's drinking coffee.

1. What's she drinking? She's drinking water.

2. What's she drinking?  She's drinking lemonade.

3. What's he drinking?  He's drinking tea.

What's she eating? She's eating bread.

1. What's he eating?  He's eating ice cream.

2. What's he eating?  He's eating meat.

3. What's she eating?  She's eating cheese.

1 Introduce

Draw two glasses and two cups on the board. Say and write:
> This is coffee/tea/water/lemonade.

Ask a student to come to the front of the class. "Give" him/her one of the items and say:
> Drink this coffee. (Show what you mean.)
> He's drinking coffee. (as student "drinks")

Demonstrate with the other drinks. If errors are made, point out that none of the nouns has an article here. Have the class repeat after you in **chorus.** *She's drinking coffee/tea/water/lemonade.*

2 Practice

1. **Read** (or play the tape for) the page.
2. Work with the page in the usual way, **T-C, T-S, S-S.**
3. **Pairwork.** Students should cover up the answers and try answering the questions with only the picture cues for help.

3 Follow Up

Progress Check. Draw pictures of food and drinks. Have students choose pictures at random and pantomime eating or drinking. Begin by asking one student *What's . . . (John) eating/ drinking?* Another student will answer *S(he)'s eating/drinking . . .* , and then ask a question about another student. Continue until all students have participated.

1 Introduce

Have a student come to the front. Draw a cup of coffee on the board. Have him/her "drink" the coffee as you say:

> What's s(he) doing? (Write on the board.)
> S(he)'s drinking.
> What's s(he) drinking?
> S(he)'s drinking tea.

Continue with *lemonade, water, coffee.*

2 Practice

1. **Read** (or play the tape for) the questions and answers in the box.
2. **Choral work** with the questions and answers in the first exercise.
3. **Pairwork** with the first exercise.
4. Have students write sentences that tell what the four people in the second exercise are doing.

3 Follow Up

Come back to this activity a few days later. Have students work in groups of three or four. Show them what to do with one group working at the front of the class. Write these phrases on small pieces of paper or cards and also on the board:

> drinking tea   eating ice cream   sleeping   watching TV
> eating an apple   drinking water   eating a banana   dancing

Make enough cards so that each group has a complete set. One student picks up a card , being careful not to let the others see. S(he) mimes the action and other students try to guess what s(he) is doing.

1. What's he doing?  He's drinking.

   What's he drinking? He's drinking milk.

2. What's she doing?  She's eating.

   What's she eating? She's eating fish.

What's s(he) doing?

1.

2.

3.

4.

What's she reading ? She's reading a book.

1. a letter   **2. a magazine**   **3. a newspaper**

Dick is in his room .

He's sitting on the bed.

He's eating an apple.

He's drinking milk.

He's reading a book.

Mary is in her room.

She's sitting on the rug.

She's eating a pear.

She's drinking lemonade.

She's reading a comic book .

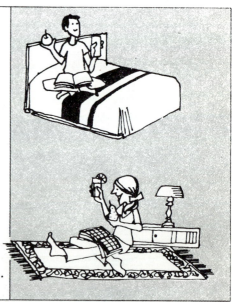

And Don?   **And Carol?**

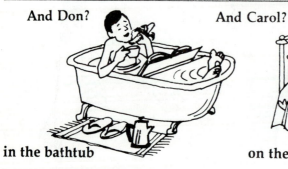

in the bathtub   **on the bed**

*54/Unit 5/*FIFTY-FOUR

1 Introduce

1. Pretend to be reading a book. Have a student come to the front. Hand him/her the book and say:

   > Read this book.
   > S(he)'s reading a book.
   > What's s(he) doing?
   > S(he)'s reading a book. (Repeat in **chorus.**)

   Continue with other students and, if possible, use a real letter, magazine, and newspaper.
2. Use the guessing game technique. Have students write their guesses on a piece of paper while you write "wrong" guesses on the board. (You may wish to write *all* the guesses on the board.)

Dick is in his room.	Where's Mary?
Where's he sitting?	What's she doing?
What's he doing?	

2 Practice

1. **Read** (or play the tape for) the model question and answer. Work **T-C** with the three substitution items.
2. Now **read** (or play the tape for) the material about Dick as students follow silently. Let students check their guesses.

   Check comprehension.

Where's Dick?	Where's Mary?
Where's he sitting?	Where's she sitting?
What's he eating?	What's she doing?
What's he drinking?	What's she drinking?
What's he reading?	What's she reading?

3. **Writing.** Discuss the pictures of Don and Carol at the bottom of the page. Have students write sentences that tell about them. Check students' work.

3 Follow Up

Have students do **Workbook** page 25.

1 Introduce

1. Put a book on a chair. Say and write on the board *There is one book on the chair*. Have students repeat in **chorus**. Continue with other objects in other places.
2. Now put two books on the chair. Practice *there are* in the same manner as above. Then say:

   There are (number) books on the chair.
   How many books are there?
   There are (number) books.
3. Take away and add books (and other objects) again to practice *there is* and *there are*.

2 Practice

1. **Read** (or play the tape for) the questions and answers—**T-C**, **T-S**, **S-S** in the usual way. Have several student **pairs** perform in front of the class.
2. **Pairwork**. Encourage students to cover the type and ask and answer the questions using only the picture for help.

3 Follow Up

1. Have students do **Workbook** pages 26, 27, and 28.
2. Write these questions on the board and explain if necessary:

   How many hours are there in a day?
   How many days are there in a week?
   How many days are there in a weekend?
   How many weeks are there in a month?
   How many days are there in a month?
3. **Pairwork.** Students ask each other these questions and answer either both with a couple of words and with a complete sentence, for example, *twenty-four hours* and *There are twenty-four hours in a day*.

How many tables are there?   There is one table.
How many lamps are there?   There are two lamps.

1. How many boys are there?   There are three boys.

2. How many guitars are there?   There are three guitars.

3. How many radios are there?   There is one radio.

4. How many lamps are there?   There are two lamps.

5. How many rugs are there?   There is one rug.

6. How many records are there?   There are four records.

7. How many chairs are there?   There are two chairs.

8. How many tables are there?   There is one table.

FIFTY-FIVE/*Unit 5/55*

Role Play

56/*Unit 5*/FIFTY-SIX

1 Introduce

1. **Read** (or play the tape for) the conversation.
2. Point as you introduce the new vocabulary words. Ask *What's this?*
3. Write *May I have some more carrots (please)?* on the board. Explain that this is a polite way to ask for something. Have students ask politely for a bus ticket, some water, that book, etc.
4. Ask students which Data Bank items are food (pepper, sugar, bread, salt, spaghetti, salad, fruit, pizza) and which are not (fork, knife, napkin, glass).
5. Tell them that forks and knives are called *utensils.* Ask them if there is another utensil mentioned in the conversation (spoon). Write *dishes, plate, bowl* on the board. Ask students if they can find a plate and a bowl in the picture at the top of the page.

2 Practice

1. **Read** (or play the tape for) the conversation again.
2. Encourage students to comment about the page. Ask students to describe the scene with sentences starting with *There is . . .* and *There are . . . .* Have them tell what people are doing.
3. Ask other questions about the picture. Work **T-C, T-S, S-S.**
4. **Pairwork.** Have students work with the entire conversation.

3 Follow Up

Role play. Students work in groups of three or more. Ask them to remember a meal they have shared recently with family or friends. Have them practice recreating that meal, and then present it to the rest of the class. As each group finishes, the other students tell who was eating, where they were, what meal they were sharing, and what food they were eating.

1 Introduce

Explain the expression *right in front of you*. Ask students questions that could be answered with expressions *right here, right there, right behind you/him/her.*

2 Practice

1. Check understanding and explain words if necessary. **Read** different lines from the conversations, for example, *Pass the bread, please.* Encourage students to respond *Here you are.*
2. Divide the class in half. Have one group read the first part in the first conversation in **chorus** while the other half responds with the second part. Switch parts and then repeat with the second conversation.
3. **Pairwork** as usual.
4. **On Your Own.** Have students work in **pairs** to role play the new situations.
5. Encourage students to extend the conversation by having students join their group as waiters or waitresses.

3 Follow Up

1. Tell students to create more specific situations. For example, you have lost your wallet with money to buy food in it. You have four friends coming for dinner and have made dinner with what food was in the house. You do not want to make your friends uncomfortable, but they keep asking for food or drink you do not have.
2. Think of other situations and write them down on cards. Come back to this page later and have students role play in small groups with the cards.

Say the Right Thing!

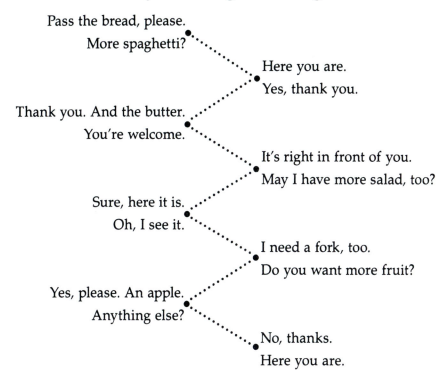

Pass the bread, please.
More spaghetti?

Here you are.
Yes, thank you.

Thank you. And the butter.
You're welcome.

It's right in front of you.
May I have more salad, too?

Sure, here it is.
Oh, I see it.

I need a fork, too.
Do you want more fruit?

Yes, please. An apple.
Anything else?

No, thanks.
Here you are.

On Your Own

Make conversations with your partner.

1. Your friend asks if you
   want more chicken.
   You say yes.
   You also want some bread.
   You also need a knife.

2. You ask your friend to
   pass the pepper.
   Your friend asks for a fork.
   You need a napkin.
   Your friend wants more
   salad.

Pronunciation

I.

nuts	socks	skirts
boots	hats	slacks
grapes	books	shorts

What's Mary eating?

Nuts and carrots.

II.

candy bars	jeans	beans
eggs	pears	shoes
chairs	girls	beds

He's eating eggs.

She's wearing red shoes.

III.

oranges	peaches	sandwiches
blouses	buses	glasses

That girl is buying two new blouses.

I'm eating peaches and oranges.

IV. Who's this?

Sue's buying oranges, pears, nuts and apples.

She's wearing red socks and white shoes.

1 Introduce

Predictable Problem. The different sounds represented by the plural markers will present difficulties for some students, especially when a "silent e" is present. Students may want to pronounce words like *names, tables, grapes* as words of two syllables. You can explain that we only pronounce the *e* when it follows a sibilant [-s] sound, [-z] sound, [-ch] sound, [-sh] sound, and [-dj] sound. Examples: *dresses, roses, peaches, radishes, judges.*

2 Practice

The final [-s], [-z], [-iz] sounds are emphasized on this page.
1. **Read** (or play the tape); students listen with books closed.
2. **Choral work** with the sentences.
3. **Pairwork.** Check pairs.

3 Follow Up

Make cards with words on them that represent all of the final [-s], [-z], [-iz] sounds, one word for each student. Pass them out. Then have students walk around the class and match their "sound' to other students' cards, that is, have them form groups with other students who have words with the same final *-s* sound.

1 Introduce

Explain carefully what students are to do: listen and write, on a separate piece of paper, the letter of the picture that best fits the dialogue.

2 Practice

1. **Read** (or play the tape for) the following:

Number 1
—Do you like grapes?   —No.
—Do you like nuts?   —Yes.
—Good. Here's a nut.

Answers
1. b, 2. b, 3. b, 4. a, 5. c

Number 2
—Where's your father?   —He's in the store.
—What's he doing?   —He's buying eggs.

Number 3
—Where's your mother?
—She's in the living room.
—What's she doing?
—She's drinking coffee.

Number 4
—Can I help you?
—Eight apples, please.
—Here you are. Anything else?
—No, thank you. How much is that?
—That's two dollars, please.

Number 5
—Six eggs and six oranges, please.
—Eggs and oranges. Here you are.
—Thank you.
—Anything else? Apples, pears?
—No, thank you.
—That's three dollars, please.

2. **Read** all five items again, pausing briefly for all students to re-examine their answers.

3 Follow Up

Have students do **Workbook** page 29.

Listen & Understand

Fast Track

Here's your room key. Room **402**.

What floor is that on, please?

The **fourth** floor.

Thank you.

You're welcome.

Now make your own conversations with a partner.

Room 509	Room 206
Room 608	Room 92
Room 57	Room 321

the first	the second	the third	the fourth
1st	2nd	3rd	4th
the fifth	the sixth	the seventh	the eighth
5th	6th	7th	8th
the ninth	the tenth	the eleventh	the twelfth
9th	10th	11th	12th

1 Introduce

1. **Read** (or play the tape for) the conversation.
2. Ask students where the conversation is taking place (hotel).
3. Write *92, 608, 321* on the board. Read these numbers as *ninety-two, six-oh-eight, three-twenty-one* or *three-two-one.* Point out that the zero in large numbers is usually read as *oh.*

2 Practice

1. Practice the conversation **T-S, S-S.**
2. **Pairwork** as usual.
3. Do **pairwork** with the substitution items. Tell students that room numbers under 100 are probably on the *ground* floor. Another word for the ground floor is the *main* floor.

3 Follow Up

1. Have students do **Workbook** page 30.
2. Have students role play checking in to the hotel. The student who plays the room clerk can invent the room number. The student who plays the guest should continue the role play by asking to use the telephone and then calling a "friend" to tell what room he is in and what floor it is on.

A. Circle the correct words.

1. He's   eating / wearing / drinking   a pear.

2. She's   eating / reading / sitting   a newspaper.

3. He's sitting   behind / in / on   the rug.

4. She's   reading / drinking / doing   milk.

B. Complete with _a, an_, or nothing.

1. She's buying _____ apple.
2. They're drinking _____ tea.
3. I'm eating _____ egg.
4. He's buying _____ banana.

C. Write the correct questions.

1. _____ There are three boys.

2. _____ There is one guitar.

3. _____ There is one lamp.

4. _____ There are two chairs.

5. _____ There is one table.

Review/Enrich

1. Write the following *-ing* phrases on separate pieces of paper or cards:

sitting on the floor	eating an apple	eating ice cream
sitting on the table	eating a banana	drinking coffee/tea
buying a book	drinking lemonade	reading a letter

   Call a student to the front of the room. Give the student one of the *-ing* phrase cards. The student will read silently and pantomime the action. Ask the class *What's s(he) doing?* Let students guess. Repeat with others.

2. The **box drill** technique provides endless and enjoyable opportunities for review. Try this one to review or culminate the work so far on the present progressive. Tell students they are at a party. Be sure they understand they can answer the questions you are going to ask any way they like. Begin by asking *Who's at the party?* (*John*), *What's he doing?* (*eating a sandwich*), *Where is he?* (*on the sofa*).

   Add students' suggestions to the board, and continue the questioning until you have five to ten people "doing" something at the party.

   THE PARTY

WHO	WHAT	WHERE
John	eating a sandwich	on the sofa
Mary	sitting	in an armchair
Sam	sleeping	under the table

Begin with alternative questions.	*Is Mary or John on the sofa?*
Follow with yes/no questions.	*Is Sam sleeping in a chair?*
Finish with information questions.	*Who's eating a sandwich?*

   If you think your students can handle it, ask more challenging questions:
   Ask me if . . . (*John is sleeping*).
   Ask me anything you like. (Give some false answers to keep students alert.)
   The answer is "sleeping." What's the question? (What's Sam doing?)
   The answer is "on the sofa." What's the question? (Where's John?)
   (etc.)

   Box drills are effective and fun. They can be used to drill any tense. Simply present a situation like the party in the tense you want to work with—*We were at a party last week* (past and past progressive); *going to a party tomor-row night* (simple future); *have just arrived at a party* (present perfect), etc.

Objectives

Communication
Identifying: *occupations, nationalities, ages, names, books*
Inquiring/Reporting: *quantity*

Grammar
is/are/am + predicate adjective/predicate noun
singular/plural nouns + *there is, there are*
irregular plural nouns
review of noun plural final sounds [-s], [-z], [-iz]
short answers with *I am, I'm not*

Vocabulary/Expressions

				Data Bank
accountant	day	nurse	teacher	cooking
age	doctor	occupation	teeth	gardening
airport(s)	engineer	only	theater(s)	music
am	every	other	tooth	snakes
architect	executive	passport	traffic	sports
army officer	far	people	train	
baby(ies)	feet	pilot	village	
bank(s)	flight attendant	police station	waiter	
bridge(s)	foot	pollution	want	
brush(es)	from	post office	weeks	
buildings	garages	secretary	women	
bus station	good	small	Fine.	
but	here	square	How about you?	
card	hotel(s)	staying	How are you?	
cemetery(ies)	how long	still	in the middle of	
check out	lawyer	strawberry(ies)	in the morning	
chef	libraries	student	No, I'm not.	
child	many	supermarket(s)	Not bad.	
church(es)	men	take out	That's all.	
control	nationality	taxi driver	That's right.	
country(ies)	noise			

Introduce the Unit

1. **Read** the dialogue; students repeat in **chorus.** Use pictures of a student, a teacher, and a doctor. Hold up the picture of the student and ask *Is this a doctor?* Students answer *no*; hold up the picture of the teacher (no). Hold up the correct one. Write each word as students choose the pictures.
2. **Pairwork** with the dialogue.

6

—Tom! Hello, how *are* you?
— Fine Rita. How are *you*?
— Not bad. Are you still a student?
—No, I'm a teacher now. How about you?
—I'm a doctor now.

—Are you still **a** secretary?

—No, I'm **an** executive now.

1. flight attendant   pilot

2. nurse   doctor

3. taxi driver   lawyer

4. engineer   architect

5. accountant   army officer

6. waiter   chef

1 Introduce

If you have pictures for the occupations shown here, use them in the same manner as for page 61. If you do not have pictures, teach the new words in context and with the help of the pictures in the text. Work **T-C** with new vocabulary.

2 Practice

1. Point to the pictures in the book and work **T-C** in the following manner:
   T: Number 1. Is he a doctor?
   S: No, he isn't.
   T: Is he a flight attendant? (Point to flight attendant.)
   S: Yes, he is.
   T: Number 2. Is he a chef or a nurse? (Point to nurse.)
   S: He's a nurse.
   T: Number 3. What's her occupation? (Point to taxi driver.)
   S: She's a taxi driver.
   Continue with yes-no questions, alternative questions and information questions about 4, 5 and 6.
2. Explain *still* if necessary: that a person was once a nurse, for example, but is not now. **Read** (or play the tape for) the short dialogue. Practice making questions in **chorus:** *Is s(he) still a . . . ?* (etc.)
3. Using the same questions, teach *now* by asking and answering:
   Is s(he) still a . . . ?
   No, s(he)'s a . . . now.
4. Work **T-C, T-S, S-S** with all the pictures.

3 Follow Up

1. Have students do **Workbook** pages 31 and 32.
2. **Pairwork.** Ask students what their occupations are. Have them substitute their occupations in the dialogue at the top of the page. Then have them ask questions about each other similar to the ones in number 1 above. Keep in mind the idea that every student should do as much oral work as possible, and do not be disturbed by what may seem like too much "noise" in the classroom.

1   Introduce

(Books closed) Write these nationalities on the board and beside them write the names of their corresponding countries:

Vietnamese—Vietnam   Chinese—China, Hong Kong, Taiwan
American—United States   Mexican—Mexico
Brazilian—Brazil   Colombian—Colombia

Read the nationalities and countries and have students repeat. Then say *A Vietnamese person is from Vietnam. An American is from the United States. A Brazilian is from Brazil. A Chinese person is from China or Hong Kong or Taiwan. A Mexican is from Mexico. A Colombian is from Colombia.*

2   Practice

1. **Read** (or play the tape for) the first three questions and answers as students follow silently. Students should have no problem with *No, I'm not.*
2. **Choral work** with all the questions and answers at the top of the page.
3. Play a guessing game. Tell students that you are one of the people in the boxes. They must ask you questions and guess which person you are.
   If you choose to be Robert Chan, for example, the questioning should go something like this:
   - **S:** Are you Chinese?
   - **T:** Yes, I am.
   - **S:** Are you 64?
   - **T:** No, I'm not.
   - **S:** Are you 80?
   - **T:** Yes, I am.
   - **S:** Are you a waiter?
   - **T:** Yes, I am.
   - **S:** You're Robert Chan!
   - **T:** That's right.

   Allow the student who guesses who you are to be the "teacher." Let students guess who s(he) is.
4. **Pairwork** or form groups of four, working as above.

3   Follow Up

Predictable Problem Students may still be having trouble using *he's* and *she's* correctly. Give students the name of a person in one of the boxes, and have students make statements about him/her using *he's* or *she's*:
   - **T:** Dr. Blume
   - **S:** He's Brazilian. He's fifty-seven. He's a doctor.

You can also do this with statements about students in the class.

1. Are you Colombian?   No, I'm not.
   Are you Mexican?   No, I'm not.
   Are you American?   Yes, I am.

2. Are you twenty-six?   No, I'm not.
   Are you nineteen?   Yes, I am.

3. Are you a taxi driver?   No, I'm not.
   Are you a student?   Yes, I am.

4. You're Nancy Novak!   That's right.

Vietnamese 28 accountant Huynh Nhuong	American 36 chef Nak Choung	Vietnamese 44 teacher Hung Phan
Brazilian 57 doctor Dr. Blume	Chinese 64 teacher Karen Wu	Mexican 32 secretary Marta Sanchez
American 18 taxi driver Mario Martini	Brazilian 27 army officer General Branco	Mexican 19 flight attendant Margarita Gonzalez
Colombian 70 architect Elena Silva	American 19 student Nancy Novak	Chinese 80 waiter Robert Chan

PASSPORT CONTROL

—Good morning.
—Good morning. What's your name, please?
—My name is **Pat Goldman.**
—Are you **American?**
—Yes, I am.
—How old are you?
—I'm **twenty-six.**
—And what's your occupation
—I'm **a doctor.**
—How long are you staying?
—Two weeks.
—Thank you. That's all.
—Thank *you.* Good-bye.

NAME	NATIONALITY	AGE	OCCUPATION
1. Pat Goldman	American	46	doctor
2. Roberto Flores	Mexican	53	teacher
3. John Cooper	English	39	secretary
4. Maria Tiant	Puerto Rican	29	pilot
5. Miguel Pinto	Venezuelan	60	executive
6. Aki Hiroshi	Japanese	72	accountant

1 Introduce

Introduce new nationalities on this page by writing them on the board with their country and making sentences in the same manner as for page 63:

English—England   Venezuelan—Venezuela
Puerto Rican—Puerto Rico   Japanese—Japan

2 Practice

1. **Read** (or play the tape for) the passport control dialogue in **chorus.** You may have to explain *How long are you staying?*
2. Work **T-C, T-S, S-S** with the dialogue.
3. Have students substitute the people in the box for Pat Goldman.
4. **Pairwork** with the substitution items. Switch. Check pairs.

3 Follow Up

1. Have students do **Workbook** page 33.
2. Ask for volunteers to play the part of the customs officer and a traveler (Pat Goldman or any name from the boxes) without looking at their books. Do not insist on a perfect recreation of the dialogue. Supply explanations if students want to use words that are not in the book.

1 Introduce

Note: Quite a few new vocabulary words are presented on this page, but all are clearly defined by the pictures. Take time going through your presentation.

1. Review some familiar nouns which add -s to form their plurals.

apple—apples	student—students
skirt—skirts	pilot—pilots
boy—boys	book—books

Have students recall [-s] and [-z] sounds of the -s endings.
2. Demonstrate the following spelling change with familiar words. Write and say:

secretary—secretaries	baby—babies
nationality—nationalities	library—libraries

Choral work with the words on the board.

2 Practice

1. **Read** (or play the tape for) the dialogue in the box at the top of the page. Work **T-C**, **T-S**, **S-S** with the substitution items.
2. **Read** (or play the tape for) the second boxed dialogue. Work **T-C**, **T-S**, **S-S** with the substitution items.
3. **Pairwork** with the entire page.

3 Follow Up

Progress Check Pronounce the following plural words and have students raise one hand when they hear the [-s] sound and two hands when they hear the [-z] sound:

apples [-z]	architects [-s]	pilots [-s]	libraries [-z]
countries [-z]	chefs [-s]	boys [-z]	babies [-z]
books [-s]	doctors [-z]		

—Is there one bank,
 or are there two **banks** here?
—There are two **banks**.

1. supermarket

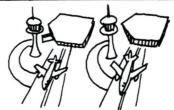

2. airport

3. hotel

4. theater

—Is there one **library**,
 or are there two libraries here?
—There are two **libraries**.

1. cemetery (cemeteries)

2. baby (babies)

3. strawberry (strawberries)

4. country (countries)

—Is there one garage,
  or are there two **garages** here?
—There are two **garages**.

1. church (churches)

2. sandwich (sandwiches)

2. bridge (bridges)

4. brush (brushes)

—Is there one **man**,
  or are there two men here?
—There are two **men**.

1. woman (women)

2. child (children)

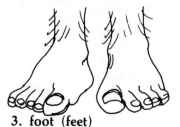

3. foot (feet)

4. tooth (teeth)

66/Unit 6/SIXTY-SIX

1 Introduce

1. Use your own pictures to practice the noun plurals presented on pages 65 and 66. Stress pronunciation changes that occur.
   Ask students to tell you how the following forms are different from -s, -es, or -ies plurals. Show pictures as you say and write:

   woman—women   foot—feet
   child—children   tooth—teeth

2. Work **T-C**, **T-S** with the words on the board. Pay special attention to the pronunciation of *woman/women*.

2 Practice

1. **Read** (or play the tape for) the first dialogue in the box at the top of the page. Work **T-C**, **T-S**, **S-S** with the substitution items.
2. **Read** (or play the tape for) the second boxed dialogue. Work **T-C**, **T-S**, **S-S** with the substitution items.
3. **Pairwork** with the entire page.

3 Follow Up

Have students do **Workbook** page 34.

Predictable Problem. Students may have difficulty with the pronunciation changes in the singular and the plural forms. Students may pronounce the *i* in *child* and *children* identically. Also, it is often difficult for students to hear the sound changes in *woman/women*. Even though the spelling change is in the second syllable, pronunciation changes occur in both the first and the second syllable. The *-oo-* spelling in *foot* and *tooth* may cause students to think they are pronounced the same.

Show and practice *foot* with *book, tooth/school/noon, cook/look/good, boots/room/too*.

1 Introduce

1. Explain to students that they are going to read a story about a village. Write *far*, *square*, *buildings* on the board and explain.
2. Prepare students to find the answers to these two questions:

   Is the village near New York or Manchester? (Explain *near*.)
   How many churches are there?

2 Practice

1. **Read** (or play the tape for) the story without stopping.
2. This is the first long narrative the students encounter. Discuss and practice it in the following manner.
   a. Read the first two sentences. Discuss any unfamiliar words.
   b. Read them again and have students "whisper" the text while you read.
   c. **Choral work**.
   d. Students read in half-voice independently.

   Read a few lines at a time in the above manner. Emphasize the rising intonation for words and phrases in a series: *a bank, the post office, the bus station, the police station*.
3. Work **T-S, S-S** with the questions at the end of the story.

3 Follow Up

In a few days, come back to the story and the questions at the bottom of the page. Have students pretend they are in a bus station and they are asking a fellow traveler about the village they come from. Do **pairwork** as follows:

   S1:   Where is . . . ?
   S2:   It's not far from . . . .
   S1:   How many buses are there to . . .?
   S2:   There are . . . buses every day.

It is not necessary that students remember the exact questions or ask them in the same order as the book. Encourage them to think of real villages that they have lived in or visited. If some students have never seen a small village, encourage other students to describe the villages they know. Use the vocabulary on the page or supply other vocabulary.

Greenfield is a small village in England. It's not far from Manchester. There are five buses to Manchester every day, but there is only one train. There aren't many people on the train at six o'clock in the morning.

The church is in the middle of the village on the square. There are many other buildings on the square. There is a bank, the post office, the bus station and the police station. The library is behind the police station.

There are two garages in front of the bridge. There is a small cemetery behind the church. It's a small village, isn't it? There is no traffic, no noise, and no pollution.

1. Where is Greenfield?
2. How many buses are there to Manchester?
3. Are there many people on the train?
4. What is in the middle of the village?
5. What other buildings are on the square?
6. Where's the library?
7. What are there in front of the bridge?
8. What's behind the church?

Role Play

May I help you?

Yes, please. I'm looking for a book about cooking.

Here are some good books.

How many can I take out?

You can check out three.

I want these, please.

May I have your library card?

Here it is.

Data Bank

GARDEN

COOKING

SNAKES

SPORTS

music

1 Introduce

1. Ask students where this conversation takes place (in a library); what you call a person who works in a library (a librarian); and the verb that means to take a book out of the library (check out a book).
2. **Read** (or play the tape for) the conversation.
3. (Books closed) Ask students the following questions to see how much they remember:

   Who is helping the woman? (the librarian)
   What is she looking for? (a book about cooking)
   How many books can she check out? (three books)
   What does she need (to check books out)? (a library card)

2 Practice

1. **Read** (or play the tape for) the conversation again.
2. Work **T-C, T-S, S-S** as usual with pairs of lines from the conversation.
3. **Pairwork.** Have students work with the entire conversation.
4. Discuss the kinds of books in the Data Bank. Ask students if they are interested in any of them. Ask them why or why not.
5. **Role play.** Have students work in pairs with this conversation. Tell them to choose various books from the Data Bank or their own favorites.

3 Follow Up

Encourage students to talk about other types of books in a library. Write the suggestions on the board. Ask students what other questions they might ask a librarian. (*Where is the copy machine? How can I get a library card?*, etc.)
Then have students work in groups of three or four to improvise conversations from the questions. Suggest that they let other students play the parts of family members or friends.

1 Introduce

If possible, display books from different libraries. Ask *Where are these books from?* Students examine the books to find the name of the library they belong to. Ask students if they know the names of local libraries. If they belong to a library, ask them which one they belong to. Ask students with library cards to show them to you and the rest of the class. Ask them where the library is located and how they get there (by bus, etc.).

2 Practice

1. Students help you put together the first conversation. Have them work in groups of three of four to find the right responses. Appoint one person in the group to be the secretary and write down the conversation.
2. **Read** the first conversation. Students check their own work.
3. Repeat 1 and 2 for the second conversation.
4. **Pairwork** as usual.
5. **On Your Own.** Have students work in **pairs** to role play the new situations.
6. A student repeats a line from one of his/her conversations. Another student in the class suggests a next line. The class decides if it is a good response. (It does not matter if it is the same as the original one or not.)

3 Follow Up

Write all of the sentences from the two conversations on the top of the page on strips of paper. (You can always have students create their own sentence strips in one class, and then come back to the activity the next class.) Keep the sentences in sets so that they don't get mixed up. Have students work in groups of three or four to assemble their conversation as quickly as possible. They can find another group with the other conversation and exchange sets.

Say the Right Thing!

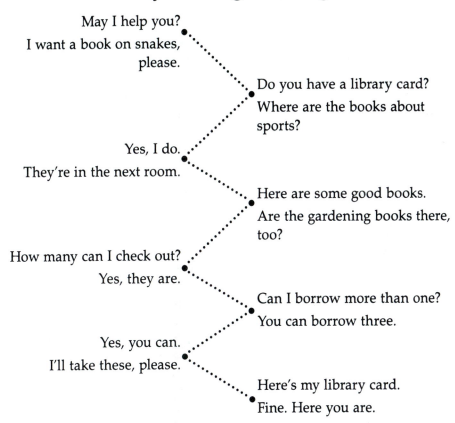

May I help you?

I want a book on snakes, please.

Do you have a library card?

Where are the books about sports?

Yes, I do.

They're in the next room.

Here are some good books.

Are the gardening books there, too?

How many can I check out?

Yes, they are.

Can I borrow more than one?

You can borrow three.

Yes, you can.

I'll take these, please.

Here's my library card.

Fine. Here you are.

On Your Own

Make conversations with your partner.

1. You ask the librarian for a book about gardening.
   You check out two books.
   You say thank you and good-bye.

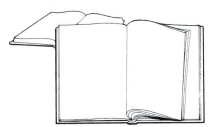

2. You're interested in books on music.
   The librarian asks if you have a card.
   You say yes.
   You choose three books.
   The librarian hopes you'll enjoy them.

1 Introduce

Read (or play the tape for) the poem. Explain anything that students do not understand. Ask students to find words in the poem that refer to parts of the body (*tails, faces, chins,* etc.) and make a list on the board. Draw a large mouse on the board and have students come up and draw lines to connect the name of the body part to the drawing.

2 Practice

1. Go through the poem **T-C.** The class can read the poem in **chorus.** Have them work in small groups to find the pairs of words that rhyme (*mice/nice, small/all,* etc.)
2. **Read** the poem line by line as you clap out the rhythm. Students repeat. Ask students to tell you how many stresses each line gets in the poem (2).
3. Have students each memorize one or more lines of the poem. Then have them recite the poem in "relay."

3 Follow Up

1. Ask students if mice are large or small (small); then ask them if the lines of the poem are short or long (long). Suggest that the short lines make you think of small animals. Ask *Which lines tell you mice are not usually people's favorite animal? (And no one seems/To like them much.)* Ask them if they like mice. Then ask them if they like the poem and why or why not.
2. **Writing.** Ask students to give you the names of some other animal or insect that people may not like. Ask why people might not like that animal/insect. Have the class work together or in small groups to write a short poem about an animal/insect from the list. Help them choose appropriate rhyming words.

Read and Enjoy

MICE

I think mice
Are rather nice.

    Their tails are long,
    Their faces small,
    They haven't any
    Chins at all.
    Their ears are pink,
    Their teeth are white,
    They run about
    The house at night.
    They nibble things
    They shouldn't touch
    And no one seems
    To like them much.

But I think mice
Are nice.

Rose Fyleman

Listen & Understand

1 Introduce

Explain carefully what students are to do: listen and write, on a separate piece
of paper, the letter of the picture that best fits the dialogue or description.

2 Practice

1. **Read** (or play the tape for) the following:

Number 1

My name is Gloria Caldo, I'm twenty-nine years
old and I'm a teacher.

Answers

1. a, 2. a, 3. b, 4. b, 5. b

Number 2

My name is Wayne Wong. I'm twenty-one years
old and I'm an architect.

Number 3

—What's your name?

—Jack Novak.

—How old are you?

—Thirty-two.

—Occupation?

—Army officer.

—Okay, thank you.

Number 4

—Bill!

—Marta! Good to see you again. How are you?

—I'm fine. How are you?

—Fine.

—Are you still a student, or are you an engineer?

—No, I'm still a student.

Number 5

My name is Mario Martini. I'm nineteen years old. I'm a student,
but I'm also a taxi driver.

2. **Read** all five items again, pausing briefly for all students to re-examine their
answers.

3 Follow Up

Have students do **Workbook** page 35.

1   Introduce

1. **Read** (or play the tape for) the conversation.
2. Have students work in **pairs** to review ordinal numbers. One student points to a day on the calendar in their book and says the month and the number, e. g., *July twelve.* The other student replies *July the twelfth* or *the twelfth of July.*

2   Practice

1. **Read** (or play the tape for) the conversation again.
2. Practice the conversation **T-S, S-S.**
3. Do **pairwork** with the substitution items. If students are having trouble remembering their "information" while they are role playing, have them make cue cards. If possible, have the pairs sit back to back as they practice, gesture picking up the telephone, etc.

3   Follow Up

1. Have students do **Workbook** page 36.
2. The conversations on this page are quite difficult, but we all have to make appointments over the telephone at some time or another. Tell students to practice *really* listening to the other person as they give and get information. Encourage them to repeat the time and day so they can verify it. Have them practice writing it down as they hear it for the first time. Show them how to ask the other person to wait a minute while they write. Come back to this page later to review material in Unit 10.

Fast Track

—**Dr. Fisher's office.**

—Hi. I'd like to make an appointment.

—Okay. How about **Friday July 27th at 9:15?**

—Fine.

—I need your home phone number, please.

—**432-6692**.

—That's **Friday July 27th at 9:15.**

—Thank you. See you then!

Make these appointments.

JULY

SUN.	MON.	TUES.	WED.	THURS.	FRI.	SAT.
1 first	2 second	3 third	4 *Dr. Johnson 11:45* fourth	5 fifth	6 sixth	7 seventh
8 eighth	9 ninth	10 *Beautiful Hair 4:00* tenth	11 eleventh	12 twelfth	13 thirteenth	14 fourteenth
15 fifteenth	16 sixteenth	17 seventeenth	18 eighteenth	19 *Tax accountant 3:00* nineteenth	20 twentieth	21 twenty-first
22 twenty-second	23 *Sunshine Travel 10:30* twenty-third	24 twenty-fourth	25 twenty-fifth	26 twenty-sixth	27 *Dr. Fisher 9:15* twenty-seventh	28 twenty-eighth
29 twenty-ninth	30 thirtieth	31 *Employment Agency 12:00* thirty-first				

Unit Six Test

A. Write the correct questions.

1. _____ No, I'm American.

2. _____ No, I'm thirty-two.

3. _____ I'm a secretary.

4. _____ I'm staying two weeks.

B. Write the correct questions.

1. _____ There are two babies.

2. _____ There is one cemetary.

3. _____ There is one church.

4. _____ There are three women.

C. Fill in the missing words.

Greenfield _____ a small village _____ England. It is not

_____ from Manchester. There _____ five buses

_____ Manchester every day, but _____ is only one train.

There are not _____ people on the train _____ six o'clock

_____ the morning. The church is _____ the middle

_____ the village _____ the square.

There are two garages in _____ of the bridge. It's a small village.

There _____ no traffic, _____ noise _____ no

pollution.

Review/Enrich

1. **Guided Composition.** Have each student create an imaginary person and answer the following questions on paper. Encourage students to use vocabulary they already know, but be willing to provide any new words/translation they need.

   What's your name? What's your nationality?
   How old are you?
   What's your occupation?
   What's your favorite color?
   What color is your hair/shirt/blouse?
   What color are your eyes/shoes/etc.?
   Are you tall or short?

   Have volunteers read their descriptions to the rest of the class. You may also wish to have students re-ask and answer the above guiding questions after each reading.

2. **Dictation.** Dictate some short sentences and have students supply answers for any questions.

   a. This is my friend, Tom.
   b. How are you?
   c. Is Rita still a doctor?
   d. Are you still a student?
   e. Are you Mexican?
   f. Do you like apples?

3. **Game.** Play an alphabet game around the room. Write the alphabet on the board. The first student must say a word beginning with *a* (apple, architect, etc.), the second with *b* (boy, banana, bed), and so on. A student who cannot think of a word within 10 to 15 seconds must drop out. You may want to cross out *q, v, x, k, u,* and *z* from the alphabet on the board, since these are difficult for most students. Students should know enough words at this point to play the game several times without repeating words.

4. **Song.** Use the model teaching plan on page 279 to introduce the song "This Land is Your Land." Words and activities for the song are on page 282.

More Communicative Practice

1. Have **pairs** conduct interviews. Have students supply information about real people they know and write it on the board. For example:

   Maria (or Eduardo) Sanchez
   27 years old
   architect

2. Have students tell or write about themselves in seven sentences or so.

Objectives

Communication
Inquiring/Reporting: *identifying family members/relationships; where people are/what people are doing; identifying parts of the body, health/illnesses*

Grammar
review present progressive, prepositions
singular nouns + *'s*
interrogative pronoun *which*
negative contractions

Vocabulary/Expressions

				Data Bank
all	family	knee	toe	backache
ankle	father	leg	waiting for	cold (n.)
arm	finger	listening to	washing	cough
awful	friends	mother	which	headache
bad	granddaughter	nose	wife	stomachache
back	grandfather	our	work	toothache
bathroom	grandson	parents	wrist	
brother(s)	has	sister	years old	
chest	head	son	years old	
cooking (v.)	hip	sore		
computer game	housewife	stomach	at home	
daughter	hurts	terrible	Come on over.	
ear	husband	throat	How are you feeling?	
elbow	kitchen	thumb	I'm sorry to hear that.	
			Not so good.	
			too sick	
			What's the matter with . . . ?	

Introduce the Unit

1. **Read** (or play the tape for) the dialogue. Use the picture to explain the new words.
2. Work in two groups, and then in **chorus,** with the dialogue.

7

—Come on over, Gloria.
  All our friends are here.
—Is Joe there?
—Yes, he is. He's playing the guitar.
—Are Tom and Betty there?
—Yes, they are. They're dancing.
—Is Nancy there?
—Yes, she is. She's singing.
—Is David there?
—Yes, he is. He's waiting for you!

SEVENTY-THREE/*Unit 7*/73

THE JOHNSON FAMILY

The Parents

Patricia Johnson (Pat)
mother
wife
48

Thomas Johnson (Tom)
father
husband
45

The Children

Thomas Johnson, Jr. (Tommy)
son
brother
15

Susan Johnson (Susie)
daughter
sister
21

I'm Pat Johnson. I'm a housewife. My husband's name is Tom. He's a chef. I'm forty-eight years old. Tom is forty-five. Tommy is my son. He's fifteen. Susie is my daughter. She's twenty-one. Tommy is still a student. Susie is an accountant.

1. Who is Tommy's father?	Thomas Johnson is.
2. Who is Tommy's sister?	Susie is.
3. Who is Tom's wife?	Patricia Johnson is.
4. Who is Pat Johnson's son?	Tommy is.
5. Who is a housewife?	Pat is.
6. Who is a chef?	Tom is.
7. Who are the Johnson children?	Tommy and Susie are.
8. Who are Susie's parents?	Patricia and Thomas Johnson are.

1 Introduce

(Books closed)

1. Draw four faces on the board and have students label them *father, mother, son,* and *daughter.* Then say the following sentences, and have the class repeat in **chorus:**

This is the father	This is the son
This is the mother	This is the daughter
They are the parents.	They are the children

2. Write *family* in large letters above the faces as you say:
    This is a family: two parents and two children.
3. Then label the son and daughter *Tommy* and *Susie.* Point to the father as you say:
    This is Tommy's father. This is Susie's father.
4. Point to the mother as you say:
    This is Tommy's mother. This is Susie's mother.

2 Practice

1. **Read** the captions for the pictures of the Johnson family, and have the students repeat in **chorus.** Go back to the board, and add the labels *brother, sister, wife,* and *husband* to your family.
2. **Read** (or play the tape for) the short paragraph to the students; students read again in **chorus.**
3. Work **T-S** with the questions. Point out the *'s* in *Tommy's,* etc.
4. **Pairwork** with the questions and answers.

3 Follow Up

Progress Check. Have the class look at only the top half of the page and try to answer the questions about the Johnsons. Write on the board the questions at the bottom of the page.

Culture Capsule. Note also the derivation of the name *Johnson.* It means "son of John." Some English family names, such as Williamson and Richard-son, were formed in the same manner. Ask students if they can think of any other classes of English family names. (Family names like Brown, White, Black, and Green are colors. Names like Baker, Miller, and Tinker are occupations.)

1 Introduce

1. Have one student come to the front of the class and have students guess his/her age, using *are you . . . ?* question forms. (Students may choose not to tell their real ages—let them know that they can say any age.)
2. Have students proceed with *Are you . . . ?* questions.
   If you have a male and a female in front of the class, write:

brother and sister	husband and wife	friends
father and daughter	mother and son	

   If you have students of the same sex in front of the class, write:

brothers	sisters	friends

Predictable Problem. Students should be aware that the pronoun *you* serves as either a singular or a plural form: *yous* does not exist. In *Are you brothers?* the *-s* at the end of *brothers* shows that the *you* is plural.

2 Practice

1. **Read** (or play the tape for) the conversation.
2. Practice the dialogues in **chorus**. Call attention to the negative contractions *we're not, they're not,* and *I'm not.*
3. **Pairwork** with the dialogues.

3 Follow Up

1. Have students do **Workbook** pages 37 and 38.
2. Have students bring in pictures of their families. In small groups, have them ask questions to find out the names, ages, and occupations of these people. For example: *Is your father's name . . . ? Is he forty-eight? Is he a bus driver?*, etc.
   If the students cannot guess correctly after a few tries, a student can write the answers on the board. The completed model could look like this:

father	mother	brother	sister
Pedro	Maria	Jorge	Tina
42	39	17	13
doctor	housewife	student	student

Culture Capsule. In the United States, extended families are not the norm. Grandparents may live in their own homes, in retirement communities, or in nursing homes—usually not with their children or grandchildren. How does this compare with the typical family unit in your students' culture?

1. —Are you eighteen?
   —No, I'm not.
   —Are you nineteen?
   —Yes, I am.

2. —Are you mother and daughter?
   —No, we're not.
   —Are you grandmother and granddaughter?
   —Yes, we are.

3. —Are you husband and wife?
   —No, we're not.
   —Are you brother and sister?
   —No, we're not.
   —Well, are you father and daughter?
   —Yes, we are.

4. —Are they brother and sister?
   —No, they're not.
   —Are they husband and wife?
   —No, they're not.
   —Are they mother and son?
   —Yes, they are.

5. —Are you father and son?
   —No, we're not.
   —Are you brothers?
   —No, we're not.
   —Are you friends?
   —Yes, we are.
   We're good friends.

6. —Are you the grandfather?
   —No, I'm not.
   —Are you the father?
   —No, I'm not.
   —Well, what *are* you?
   —I'm the grandson!

head
nose
ear
tooth
wrist
throat
stomach
chest
knee
elbow
arm
leg
thumb
finger
back
hip
ankle
foot
toe

—How is your mother?
—Not so good.
—What's the matter with her?
—She has a bad back.
—How is your father?
—Awful.
—What's the matter with *him*?
—He has a bad knee.
—Well, how are you?
—Terrible!
—What's the matter with *you*?
—My tooth hurts.

76/Unit 7/SEVENTY-SIX

1 Introduce

Use the picture in the book to introduce vocabulary for parts of the body.

2 Practice

1. **Read** (or play the tape for) the dialogue. Students will follow silently. Explain any new vocabulary.
2. Work **T-C**, **T-S**, **S-S** with the dialogue and substitution items.
3. **Pairwork**. Encourage students to pantomime aches in various parts of their bodies.

3 Follow Up

1. Have students do **Workbook** page 39.
2. English uses words for parts of the body in expressions like *to have or not have enough leg room* sitting on an airplane or in a theater. But sometimes expressions that contain parts of the body have nothing to do with your body or your health. Students may have heard of some of them, for example, calling someone a *pain in the neck* when s(he) annoys you.

   See if students can guess some of these. Write the expressions and their meanings on separate pieces of paper or cards, a set for each group. Have students work in groups of three or four to match the expression and the meaning.

to get off on the wrong foot	*to make an unfavorable impression*
knee high to a grasshopper	*very young*
right under your nose	*in front of you or near you*
to lose your head	*to get excited*
to pay lip service to	*to express insincere support of*

1 Introduction

(Books closed) Write the following telephone conversation on the board and work **T-C** and **T-S** with the class:

    T: Hello.
    S: Hello, is this (teacher's name)?
    T: Yes, it is.
    S: Hi, (teacher's name). This is (student's name).
    T: Hi, (student's name). How are you?
    S: Fine. How are you?
    T: Fine, thanks.

2 Practice

1. **Read** (or play the tape for) the telephone conversation and the substitution items. New vocabulary should be clear from the pictures.
2. Work **T-C**, **T-S** with the substitution items.
3. **Pairwork**.

3 Follow Up

Progress Check. Ask each student to find at least one picture (in a magazine, newspaper) showing any of the known verbs (playing, dancing, eating, drinking, singing, reading, watching TV, listening to records/the radio). Let students ask and answer questions about what the people pictured are doing. Each student can answer questions about his/her picture(s), and exchange with classmates.

—Hello.
—Hello, is this Tom?
—Yes, it is.
—Hi, Tom. This is Juan.
 How are you?
—Fine, how are *you?*
—Fine, thanks. What are you doing?
—Ben is here. We're **watching TV.**
 Come on over.

1. reading

2. listening to records

3. drinking coffee

4. playing the guitar

5. eating sandwiches

6. listening to the radio

SEVENTY-SEVEN/*Unit 7/77*

1. Which room is she in?
   Is she in the kitchen?  Yes, she is.
   What's she doing? She's cooking.

2. Which room is he in?
   Is he in the bathroom?  Yes, he is.
   What's he doing? He's reading a book.

3. Which room are you in?
   Are you in the living room? No, I'm not.
   Where *are* you? I'm in the bedroom.
   What are you doing? I'm watching TV.

4. Which room is she in?
   Is she in the kitchen?  No, she's not.
   Where *is* she? She's in the living room.
   What's she doing? She's listening to records.

5. Are they in the bedroom? No, they're not.
   Where *are* they? They're in the kitchen.
   What are they doing? They're eating.

1 Introduce

1. Draw a house on the board and divide it into four rooms: kitchen, bedroom, bathroom, living room. Have students repeat *kitchen* and *bathroom* in **chorus**.
2. Have students draw stick figures: a girl in the kitchen, a boy in the bathroom, a man in the bedroom, and a woman in the living room. Students should make man and woman stick figures bigger than the boy and girl. Have the class repeat *girl, boy, man,* and *woman* in **chorus** as you point to each figure.

2 Practice

1. **Read** (or play the tape for) the questions and answers.
2. Work **T-S** with the questions and answers, writing appropriate verbs on the board drawing (*cooking, reading,* etc.).
3. **Pairwork** with the questions and answers.

3 Follow Up

Make a series of statements, and have students tell you if you are *Right* or *Wrong* after each sentence:

> The boy and girl are in the kitchen. They're eating apples.
> The man is in the bedroom. He's watching TV.
> The woman is in the living room. She's listening to records.
> The girl is in the bathroom. She's reading the newspaper.
> They boy is in the living room. He's reading a comic book.

Culture Capsule. Prepare students for the Johnson's typical, middle-class house on page 79. In the U.S. some homes are surrounded by grass and are set back from the street. Some are one-story houses (rooms all on one floor); others have two stories. There is sometimes a patio or a screened-in porch with a yard at the back of the house. There may be a garage. Emphasize that many people also live in smaller homes (apartments, two- or three-family houses, etc.) Geographic location as well as economic status determine the size and architectural style of homes in the U.S.

1 Introduce

Explain that the next exercise in the book is a story about the Johnson family, and that you want the students to guess what the story says. As students answer your questions, have them write their guesses on a piece of paper; write yours on the board. Say:

> The family is at home.
> Is Mr. Johnson in the kitchen or in the living room? (Write an answer.)
> Is Mrs. Johnson in the living room or in the bedroom?
> Is she sitting on the sofa or in an armchair?
> Is she reading a book or a newspaper?
>
> Tommy and his friend are in the yard.
> Is his friend's name Bob or Ricky?
> Are they washing the car or playing ball?
>
> Susie and her friend are in the house.
> What's her friend's name—Carol or Pat?
> Are they reading or playing a computer game?

2 Practice

1. **Read** (or play the tape for) the story through once without interruption. Students follow silently in their books.
2. Discuss and check students' guesses.
3. Students read the story with you (or the tape) in **chorus**.
4. **Pairwork** with the questions and answers. Students cover right side, left side, and finally all type.
5. Individual students describe picture to the class, covering type.

3 Follow Up

Have students do **Workbook** page 40.

Culture Capsule. Students should note that the *man* is cooking, while the *woman* is reading the newspaper. This role-reversal is becoming more common in the United States; some families share the housework and function as a team. How does this compare with male-female roles in your culture?

The Johnson family is at home. Mr. Johnson is in the kitchen. He is cooking. Mrs. Johnson is in the living room. She is sitting in an armchair. She's reading a newspaper. Tommy and his friend, Ricky, are in the yard. They are washing the car. Susie and her friend, Carol, are in Susie's bedroom. They are playing a computer game.

1. Is Mr. Johnson in the living room?

No, he isn't.
He's in the kitchen.

2. Is Mrs. Johnson in the kitchen?

No, she isn't.
She's in the living room

3. Is Mrs. Johnson reading a book?

No, she isn't.
She's reading a newspaper.

4. Are Tommy and Ricky in the kitchen?

No, they aren't.
They're in the yard.

5. Are they washing the bus?

No, they aren't.
They're washing the car.

6. Are Susie and Carol in the kitchen?

No, they aren't.
They're in Susie's bedroom.

SEVENTY-NINE/*Unit 7*/79

Role Play

How are you feeling today?

Not so good.

What's the matter?

I have a sore throat.

I'm sorry to hear that. Are you too sick to go to work?

I think so.

Well, stay in bed. I'll call your office.

Thanks, dear.

Data Bank

a toothache

a headache

a backache

a bad cough

a stomachache

a cold

1 Introduce

1. Write these words in a list on the board:
   - sore tooth
   - sore head
   - sore back
   - sore stomach

   Then say and pantomime the actions to match:
   - I have a sore tooth. I have a toothache.
   - I have a sore head. I have a headache. (etc.)

2. **Read** (or play the tape for) the conversation. Explain vocabulary, if necessary. Explain *too sick to go to work* and ask the students for more examples of *too* (adjective) to do something (*too young to drive, too old to play football, too tired to work*).

2 Practice

1. **Read** (or play the tape for) the conversation again.
2. Divide the class in half. Have them read the conversation in **chorus.** Have one half play the first character, the other half play the other character. Switch.
3. **Pairwork.** Have students work with the entire conversation.
4. Model pronunciation of the data bank vocabulary and have students repeat in **chorus.** Make sure that students pronounce correctly the k sound in *-ache.*

Follow Up

Role Play. Students work in groups of three of four to role play similar situations with different combinations of family members or friends.

1   Introduce

(Books closed)
Write *So do I.* on the board and explain.Pantomime various actions and say
what's wrong. Students can pantomime similar actions and respond as follows:

  T: I have a sore throat. (pantomiming a sore throat)
  C: So do I. (doing the same)
  T: I have a backache. (bending over and touching the back)
  C: So do I. (doing the same)
  T: I have a bad cough. (pretending to cough) (etc.)

2   Practice

1. **Read** the first line of the first conversation and ask students what should
   come next. When they have agreed on the right choice, continue with the
   rest of the conversation.
2. Introduce the second conversation the same way.
3. Check understanding by reading different lines from the conversation.
   Students respond in **chorus**; they may look in the book for appropriate
   responses.
4. Divide the class in half. Have one group **read** the first part in each conversation in **chorus** while the other half responds with the second part. Continue with the rest of the conversation and then switch parts.
5. **On Your Own.** Have students work in **pairs** to role play the new situations.

3   Follow Up

Writing. Have students copy the two conversations on the top of the page.
Check to see that they write the sentences in the proper sequence.

Say the Right Thing!

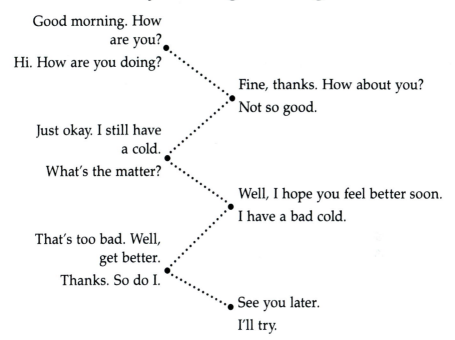

Good morning. How
are you?

Hi. How are you doing?

Fine, thanks. How about you?
Not so good.

Just okay. I still have
a cold.

What's the matter?

Well, I hope you feel better soon.
I have a bad cold.

That's too bad. Well,
get better.

Thanks. So do I.

See you later.
I'll try.

On Your Own

Make conversations with your partner.

1. Your friend doesn't come to work.
   You call your friend.
   Your friend has a cold.
   You hope your friend will be better
   soon.

2. You wake up feeling sick.
   You have a stomachache.
   You call your office.
   Your boss asks what's the
   matter.
   Your boss is sorry to
   hear it.

Pronunciation

I.

she	tea	see
green	cheese	eating
meat	please	peach
Peter	teacher	three

She's reading.

Peter's eating a green peach.

II.

six	fish	sitting
milk	drinking	in
it	is	Bill
still	English	Tim

Is Bill drinking milk?

Tim is sitting in the living room.

III.

banks	guitars	blouses
airports	records	brushes
hats	schools	watches
weeks	hotels	offices
bus	trees	churches
across	flowers	bridges

1 Introduce

The long and short vowel sounds are practiced in **I** and **II**. Be sure that students hear the differences and note the different positions of their tongues when they say the sounds. More practice in final (-s), (-z), and (-iz) sounds is given in **III**.

2 Practice

1. (Books closed) **Read** (or play the tape); students listen.
2. Do **choral work** with the sentences.
3. **Pairwork.** Go around the room checking pairs.

Predictable Problem Some students may pronounce the sounds as if they were both the long *e* sound. One remedy for this is to have the students concentrate on the corners of their mouths and try not to "smile" when saying *i* as in *six*. Another remedy is to use minimal pairs, with one known word and one new word: *meat/mitt, peach/pitch, eat/it, steal/still, ease/is, seating/sitting, team/Tim. green/grin* These words are introduced for pronunciation only. Do not try to explain them at length.

3 Follow Up

Divide the class in half. Explain that one half of the class is the "short i" group and the other half is the "long e" group. Have them practice the different vowel sounds. Then read a list of words that contain one or the other of these sounds. Students write the words that belong in their group. Then, see if they can come up with any other words that belong in their group. Have the groups exchange papers and check each others' work. Discuss any disagreements.

1 Introduce

Have students look at the pictures on the page. Then tell them they will be hearing a story about the Gianetto family.

2 Practice

This listening test is different from those which students have done up to now. Explain carefully what they are to do:

Students should:
1. Look at the choices once.
2. Listen to the paragraph and questions *without* writing.
3. Listen to the paragraph and questions again; choose answers.
4. Listen once more: check answers.

The teacher should:
1. Give students time to look at the choices.
2. **Read** (or play the tape) once.
3. **Read** again, pausing after each question.
4. **Read** a third time without pausing.

This is the paragraph to be **read** (or played on the tape):

> The Gianetto family is at home. Mr. Gianetto is in the kitchen. He is cooking. Mrs. Gianetto is in the living room. She is sitting in an armchair. She's reading the newspaper. The two boys, Ricardo and Robert, are in the yard. They are washing the car. Charles, the cat, is under a chair in the living room.

Number 1
Where is Mr. Gianetto?

Number 2
What is Mr. Gianetto doing?

Number 3
What is Mrs. Gianetto doing?

Number 4
What are the boys doing?

Number 5
Where is Charles?

Answers
1. a, 2. c, 3. a, 4. b, 5. a

3 Follow Up

Have students do **Workbook** page 41.

Listen & Understand

Fast Track

—Hi, it's me.
—Hi, nice to hear from you.
   Where are you?
—I'm in **Mexico.**
—Really? What's the weather like?
—It's **hot and sunny.** How are things
   with you?
—The same as usual. **Cold and rainy.**
   When will you be back?
—I'll be back on **Monday.**
—Okay, see you then.
—Fine. Take care!

Now make conversations with your partner.

It's sunny. It's windy. It's freezing.

It's stormy. It's foggy. It's snowing.

It's raining. It's cloudy. It's warm.

Sunday	Monday	Tuesday	Wednesday	Thursday
	Friday	Saturday	Sunday	

1 Introduce

1. **Read** (or play the tape for) the entire conversation. Explain the vocabulary if necessary. Make sure that students have interpreted the pictures of different types of weather correctly .
2. Write the words *inside* and *outside* on the board and explain. Start sentences and have students finish them in **chorus** as follows:

   T: There's sun outside. It's . . .
   C: There's sun outside. It's sunny.
   T: There's wind outside. It's . . .
   C: There's wind outside. It's windy.
   T: There are clouds outside. It's . . .
   C: There are clouds outside. It's cloudy.
   T: There's fog outside. It's . . .
   C: There's fog outside. It's foggy.

2 Practice

1. **Read** (or play the tape for) the conversation again.
2. Practice parts of the conversation **T-S, S-S.**
3. **Pairwork.** Have students work with the entire conversation.
4. Do **pairwork** with the substitution items. These substitutions are quite difficult, and students will start out using their books. So they can role play the conversations more naturally, have them write the information on small pieces of paper or cards.

3 Follow Up

1. Have students do **Workbook** page 42.
2. Students can pretend they are on vacation somewhere. They write a post card to someone back home. (If you wish, you could have a real post card for each student or ask students to bring a real post card to class.) Then have volunteers come up to the front and tell the rest of the class:

   I'm in Los Angeles. I'm writing a post card to my girlfriend. Her name is Rose. She's at home in Hong Kong. This is what I'm telling her . . . (reads post card).

A. Name the family members.

1. My parents' son is my _____ .

2. My parents' daughter is my _____ .

3. My mother's husband is my _____ .

4. My father's wife is my _____ .

5. My father's father is my _____ .

B. What are the body parts?

1. _____

2. _____

3. _____

C. Complete the conversation.

_____ 1. Where is Bob?　　　　　a. They are washing the car.

_____ 2. What is he doing?　　　　b. It's sleeping.

_____ 3. Where are the children?　c. He's in the kitchen.

_____ 4. What are they doing?　　d. He's cooking.

_____ 5. Where is the dog?　　　　e. They're in the yard.

_____ 6. What is it doing?　　　　f. It's in the living room.

Review/Enrich

1. **Game**. Divide the class into two teams. Slowly, but only once, say three nouns—*bridge, library, woman*. The first player on a team must say (or write on the board) the words in the plural form in the *same order*. Alternate until every student has a turn. The teams get one point for each correct plural given in the right sequence. The team with the most points wins.

bank, secretary, brush	church, garage, bridge
child, country, guitar	man, book, radio
foot, tooth, strawberry	bus, cemetery, theater
record, lamp, woman	village, city, supermarket

2. With students' help, create a map of an imaginary city of your own on the board. Mark the locations of *post offices, police stations, theaters, garages, churches,* etc. Begin by giving this clue: *I'm behind the church. Where am I?* The students should be able to guess that you are in the cemetery, for example. Let students give similar clues and ask *Where am I?*

3. **Game**. Have students sit in a circle. One student begins by walking to another student, pointing to a part of his/her body or clothing, and saying *This is my . . .* (something other than what s(he) is pointing to). If the student points to his/her ear, s(he) might say *This is my elbow.* The other student must say and do the reverse: point to his/her elbow and say *That is your elbow.* The player who makes a mistake takes the next turn.

More Communicative Practice

Have students write answers about themselves. If a question does not apply to them, they can put an X.

   a. Who are your parents?
   b. What's your grandmother's name?
   c. Are you seventeen years old?
   d. Who's your father's son?
   e. Who's your father's daughter?

Objectives

Communication
Inquiring/Reporting: *ownership, nationalities; shopping for clothes*

Grammar
singular/plural nouns + *'s/s'*
objective pronouns *me, you, him, her, us, them*
demonstrative pronouns *this, that, these those*
possessive adjectives *our, their*
question word *whose*

Vocabulary/Expressions

			Data Bank	
big	me	their	average	neat
circles	office	them	beautiful	petite
costume party	pencil	these	big	pretty
cup	player	those	extra-large	short
give	racket	tired	extra-long	small
gloves	roller skates	to	large	too
helping	size	us	long	ugly
him	so	whose	medium	
ice skates	squares			

This is perfect!

Introduce the Unit

Take time to review the familiar forms of nouns and pronouns before you introduce the new material.

1. Write *who, who's,* and *whose* on the board. Pronounce *whose* and emphasize that *who's* and *whose* sound alike, but that they have different spellings and meanings. Remind students that *who's* is the contraction form of *who is. Whose* is one word, and it denotes possession. Write *Mary's* on the board next to *whose* to show the connection. Say and write:

    This is Mary's book   Whose boots are these?
    Whose book is it?   (Explain)
    It's Mary's.   They're Jack's.

2. **Read** (or play the tape for) the two dialogues with students repeating in **chorus**. Work **T-S, S-T, S-S** as usual.

8

—Whose cup is this?
—It's Mary's.
—Well, give it to her.

—Whose glasses are these?
—They're Juan's.
—Well, give them to him.

EIGHTY-FIVE/Unit 8/85

1. *This* racket is old, but *that* racket is new.

2. *This* is a Canadian player, and *that* is a Mexican player.

3. *These* roller skates are Peter's, and *those* ice skates are Mary's.

4. *These* circles are big, but *those* squares are small.

1. This is an English car.　　These are Japanese cars.

2. That is a Turkish pilot.　　Those are Colombian pilots.

3. These are American footballs.　Those are Brazilian footballs.

*86/Unit 8/*EIGHTY-SIX

1 Introduce

Review *this/that* before beginning this lesson. Put a book on your desk. Touch it and say *This is a book.* Add several more books; touch them and say *These are books.* Now put one book far away from where you are standing and say *That is a book over there.* Add more books; walk away and say *Those are books over there.* Write:

1 book	this, that
2 books	these, those

Make sure students understand both the singular and plural and the difference in usage between *this/that* and *these/those*.

2 Practice

Read (or play the tape for) the entire page. Explain any unfamiliar words and work in **chorus**. Point out that *this/that, these/those* can be used with nouns or alone, for example, *This dress is orange./This is orange./ These candy bars are good./These are good.*

3 Follow Up

1. Have students do **Workbook** page 43.
2. Come back to this page after a few days. Show students how, in spoken English, statements are often turned into questions by using a rising intonation. Using the statements in the box at the top of the page, say: *This racket is old?* and have students respond *Yes, it is.* Repeat for the first part of the other three statements. Then ask and answer the same question for the first statement *This racket is old? Yes, but that racket is new.* Students do **pairwork** with the rest of the page in the same way:

S1:	This is a Canadian player?
S2:	Yes, but *that* is a *Mexican* player.
S1:	These roller skates are Peter's?
S2:	Yes, but *those ice skates* are Mary's.
S1:	These circles are big?
S2:	Yes, but *those squares* are small.

1 Introduce

Explain to students that the empty balloon means that they supply the missing words. Point to the first box and ask students *Which is your pencil?* Students respond *This is my pencil.*

2 Practice

1. Students should be able to produce responses to the first four questions, using the pictures for clues. Initially, you may need to prompt students, but they should be able to produce responses using *this, that, these,* and *those.*
2. Continue with free production for the last four boxes. Accept any reasonable statements; prompt any students who need help. Check on correct usage of *this, that, these,* and *those.*

3 Follow Up

Bring in some large newspaper or magazine pictures or advertisements showing familiar vocabulary items. Some pictures should show single items and some should show groups of similar items. For example, you could have a picture of a man in a shirt and a picture of several shirts. Put the pictures up on the board. Point to one picture and say *This is a shirt.* Point to the other picture and say *These are shirts.* Volunteers can come up to the board and do the same. Tell them they do not have to "tell the truth." They can try to fool the rest of the class. Encourage other students to tell them the correct statement.

What are they saying? Use **this, that, these** or **those** *in your answers.*

—Is this **Mr. Green's** office? —No, it isn't.
—Whose office *is* it? —It's **Ms. Pott's.**

—Is this your **shirt?** —No, it isn't.
—Whose **shirt** *is* it? —It's **Tom Marks's.**

1. sweater/Mike Jones's   4. car/Maria March's

2. hat/Betty Church's   5. boyfriend/Sally Burns's

3. tie/Dennis's   6. racket/James's

—Is this your **rug?** —No, it isn't.
—Whose **rug** *is* it? —It's **the Greens'.**

1. bedroom/the boys'   4. football/the students'

2. teacher/the girls'   5. store/the Johnsons'

3. car/the Blacks'   6. garage/the Kings'

1 Introduce

1. Quickly review the familiar *'s* possessive form

> **T**: Is this your hat? (book, pen, pencil, etc.)
> **S**: No, it isn't.
> **T**: It's Carlo's. (Continue with names of other students: write the possessive forms on the board.)

2. List a few nouns on the board. Then list:

Dennis	The Browns
Mr. Jones	the boys
James	the girls

Add *'s* to each word on the left. Pronounce the words, emphasizing the added syllable. Have students repeat in **chorus**. Now add an apostrophe only to the words on the right. Say the words slowly so students can hear one syllable only.

Predictable Problem. Students may be confused by the *'s* and the *s'*. Ask students how these two possessive forms differ. You may need to point out that *'s* is used when one person is the possessor, regardless of the ending on that person's name. It is also important to note that we add an extra syllable to singular possessives ending in *-s* or *-ch*: *James's* becomes a two-syllable word.

2 Practice

1. **Read** (or play the tape for) the dialogue at the top of the page. Work **T-C**, **T-S**, **S-S** with the substitution items in the picture.
2. **Read** (or play the tape for) the second dialogue. Point out that all the names in this exercise end with *-s* or *-ch*, and all are singular. Tell students to notice the addition of -s. Work **T-C**, **T-S**, **S-S** with the substitution items.
3. **Read** (or play the tape for) the last dialogue. Point out that all the possessive forms in this exercise are plural. Students should notice the added apostrophe. Work **T-C**, **T-S**, **S-S** with the substitution items.
4. **Pairwork** with the entire page.

3 Follow Up

Writing. Write the following nouns on the board:

Tom/sweater	the Johnson's store
boys/football	Betty Church/blouse
mother/racket	Miss Johnson/dress

Have students write a sentence making the first noun possessive. Check for correct usage of *'s* and *s'*. Review if necessary.

1 Introduce

Review the names of articles of clothing and the possessive. Point to the skirt in Bess's closet and say *Whose skirt is this? It's Bess's skirt.* Then point to the hat and say *Whose hat is this?* Students answer in **chorus.** Work **T-C** with Bess's and Mary's clothing. Then work **T-S** with the rest of the clothing at the top of the page.

2 Practice

1. **Read** the questions and answers about Dick in **chorus.** Be sure everyone understands what a "costume party" is.
2. **Pairwork** with the question and answers about Mike. Students will use the pictures to form the correct sentences.

3 Follow Up

Progress Check. Use your own pictures of clothing or use real items of clothing and ask: *Whose (bathrobe) is this? Whose (boots) are these?* Students can use classmates' names in their answers. Allow students to handle the pictures in order to elicit *this/these.*

THE COSTUME PARTY

What's Dick wearing?

1. Bess's hat

2. . . . .

3. . . . .

4. Mary's blouse

5. Bess's skirt

6. Fred's pants

7. . . . .

8. Mary's shoes

What's Mike wearing?

1. . . . .

2. . . . .

3. . . . .

4. . . . .

5. . . . .

6. . . . .

7. . . . .

8. . . . .

EIGHTY-NINE/*Unit 8/89*

I	am		me.
He	is		him.
She			her.
		tired, so Jack's helping	
We			us.
You	are		you.
They			them.

	my		me.
	his		him.
That's	her	book, so give it to	her.
	our		us.
	their		them.

—Whose **pen** is this?
—It's **Tom's.**
—Well, give it to **him.**

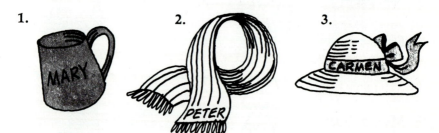

1. 2. 3.

1 Introduce

1. List the personal (nominative) pronouns *I, you, she, he, we, they* on the board. Ask volunteers to use each in a sentence.
2. Write the objective pronouns *me, him, us, you, them* next to the nominative pronouns. Ask a student to bring you his/her book. Say and write:

    This is . . . (student's name) book.

    Give it to her. (Point to a female student.)

    Repeat with another student. Say and write:

    This is . . . (student's name) book.

    Give it to him. (Point to a male student.)

    Repeat with other objects.

2 Practice

1. Work **T-C**, **T-S**, **S-S** with the two exercises.
2. **Pairwork** with the same exercises. Go around the room checking pairs.
3. **Read** (or play the tape for) the short dialogue at the bottom of the page.
4. **Pairwork** with the substitution items.

3 Follow Up

1. Have students do **Workbook** page 44.
2. **Progress Check.** Read each question twice and have students listen and write *who's* or *whose*:

    a. Who's in the bathroom?

    b. Whose book is this?

    c. Whose jeans are these?

    d. Who's cooking the eggs?

    e. Whose scarf is that?

1 Introduce

This is a review page. Read and discuss the text in the boxes. Point out that *whose* is used alone without a following noun in this exercise. Be sure every-one understands how the substitution is to be done.

2 Practice

1. **Read** (or play the tape for) the questions and answers at the top of the page.
2. Work **T-S** with the first few examples.
3. Simultaneous **pairwork** as usual.
4. Have **pairs** work orally in front of the class.

3 Follow Up

1. Have students do **Workbook** pages 45 and 46.
2. Have a student choose an object in the classroom and perform an action with it. Stand near the student and ask other students *What's this?* and *Whose is it?* (Note that the object may belong to the student who is per-forming the action or to someone else. Allow students to give the "real" answer.) Have the student ask *What am I doing?* The class answers. Then have a student ask *What is s(he) doing?* and another student answers.

Who's this?
It's Tom.

What's this?
It's a book.
Whose is it?
It's Tom's.

What's **Tom** doing?
He's reading.

1. Mary

2. James

3. Lucy

4. Mr. Dodds

5. Bess

NINETY-ONE/Unit 8/91

Role Play

May I help you?

Yes, I need a jacket.

What size do you take?

Umm, small.

Here. Try this one.

This is *too* small.

SALE

These are on sale.

How much are they?

$29.99.

Oh, this is perfect! I'll take it.

Data Bank

small	petite	ugly	too small
medium	average	beautiful	too big
large	long	pretty	too long
extra-large	extra-long	neat	too short

92/Unit 8/NINETY-TWO

1 Introduce

(Books closed) This is another page about shopping. Review clothing vocabulary by having the following conversation with yourself and then asking each student:

> **T:** I'm going shopping for clothes.
> I'm buying shoes.
> I'm buying a belt.
> (to a student) What are you buying?
> **S1:** I'm buying . . . .
> **S2:** I'm buying . . . . (etc.)

Students who need help remembering the names of items of clothing can look at page 6 of their books.

2 Practice

1. **Read** (or play the tape for) the conversation.
2. Work **T-C** with the conversation; switch roles.
3. Continue **T-S, S-S.**
4. **Data Bank.** Model the words in the Data Bank and have students repeat in **chorus.** Explain that the work *neat* does not have its normal meaning "tidy" here. It is slang for "good" or "pleasing." For example, you might say *These jeans are neat.* meaning that they please you and you like them. Activities can also be neat, as in *This party is neat* or *That movie is neat.*

3 Follow Up

Bring in advertisements (from an English-language newspaper or magazine). Tell students to scan them and take notes on the sizes, colors, styles, prices, and so on of different items. Have **pairs** of students create dialogues based on the information they have recorded.

1 Introduce

These conversations have some lines that are incomplete sentences. Write the following lines on the board and have students give you the complete sentence:

> For a boy or a girl? (Is it for a boy or a girl?)
> What size? (What size is the girl? What size do you want?)
> Any particular color? (Do you want any particular color?)

2 Practice

1. Ask students to **read** the conversation pairs silently and figure out the conversations. Remind students to notice whether the nouns are singular or plural as they figure out the correct sequencing. For example, *Here's a nice one* needs to be followed by a singular pronoun; therefore, *How much is it?* is the correct response.
2. Work **T-C, T-S** with the conversations.
3. **Pairwork.** Have students practice the conversations. Encourage them to stand up and use gestures as they pretend to show the customer the clothing and transact the sale.
4. **On Your Own. Read** the directions and the situations. Ask questions to make sure students understand the situations: *Who are you buying jeans for? Why are you looking for a present for your friend?*
5. Do **pairwork** with the situations or have students work in groups of three or four, adding other characters and extending the situations.

3 Follow Up

Writing. Have half the class write out the first conversation, beginning with *Can I help you?*—the other half write out the second conversation, beginning with *Something for you today?* Students can exchange papers to check each other's work.

Say the Right Thing!

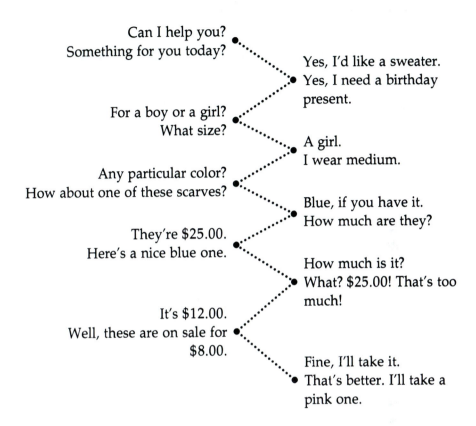

Can I help you?
Something for you today?

Yes, I'd like a sweater.
Yes, I need a birthday present.

For a boy or a girl?
What size?

A girl.
I wear medium.

Any particular color?
How about one of these scarves?

Blue, if you have it.
How much are they?

They're $25.00.
Here's a nice blue one.

How much is it?
What? $25.00! That's too much!

It's $12.00.
Well, these are on sale for $8.00.

Fine, I'll take it.
That's better. I'll take a pink one.

On Your Own

Make conversations with your partner.

1. You are shopping for yourself. You want a new pair of jeans. Tell the clerk what size you wear. Tell the clerk what color you want. Ask the price. Will you buy the jeans or not?

2. You are shopping for a present. Your friend is a boy. You see a neat record. You ask how much it is. It's too expensive. What do you buy instead?

Read and Enjoy

MY STOMACH GROWLS

My stomach growls.
My throat gurgles.
My teeth click.
My fingers crack.
My toes thump.
My nose sniffs.
My lips pop.
Even my blinks make a sound.
I'm really very noisy,
in a quiet way.

Richard J. Margolis

1 Introduce

Note: Students may notice that some of the present tense verbs end in *-s* and some do not. Do not teach the simple present tense at this time. Show them that verbs with plural subjects (teeth, fingers, etc.) end in *-s.*

Read (or play the tape for) the poem. Explain or act out anything that students do not understand. They should be familiar with the parts of the body in the poem, but the sound verbs will be difficult. Write these sound verbs on the board and then read them in a way that reflects their meaning. Ask them if any words in the poem rhyme (no). Explain that lines in poems do not *always* have to rhyme—that rhythm is important too.

2 Practice

1. **Read** the poem again line by line and exaggerate the verb sounds. Have students repeat in **chorus.**
2. Have students each memorize one or more lines of the poem. Then have them recite the poem in "relay." If some students are having trouble remembering, they can write down their line(s) . If students are missing the rhythm, have the class clap the rhythm as they recite.

3 Follow Up

Ask students if they think this is a funny poem and why. Encourage students to read the poem loudly and then softly, quickly and then slowly. Ask them if they know any other sound verbs (crash, snap, bark, crackle, tinkle, etc.).

1 Introduce

Explain carefully what students are to do: listen and write on a separate piece of paper the letter of the picture that best fits the dialogue.

2 Practice

1. **Read** (or play the tape for) the following:

Number 1
—Where's your brother?
—He's in the yard.
—Where's your sister?
—She's in the yard, too. She's washing the car.
—What's your brother doing?
—He's helping her.

Answers
1. b, 2. c, 3. b, 4. c, 5. c

Number 2
—Is this your jacket?
—No, it's Tom's.
—Give it to him please.

Number 3
—Are these my shoes?
—No they're not. Those are your shoes over there.
—Over there.
—Oh, yes. Please give them to me.

Number 4
—That's a nice blue house.   —Yes. Whose is it?
—It's the Browns' house.   —Is that their car, too?
—No, that's my car.

Number 5
—Where are the children?   —They're in the garage.
—What are they doing?   —They're cleaning it.
—Who's helping them?   —The dog!

2. **Read** all five items again, pausing briefly for all students to re-examine their answers.

3 Follow Up

Have students do **Workbook** page 47.

Listen & Understand

Fast Track

—Hi! I think I'm lost.

—Hi there! Where are you?

—I'm in **Topsfield** now. How do
I get to **Rockport?**

—Take **Route 1 South to Route 95.**
Then take **Route 128 North all the
way to Rockport.**

—Thanks. I'll call if I get lost *again!*

Give your friend directions.

Braintree ⟶ Boxford   Natick ⟶ Boston
Peabody ⟶ Lawrence   Lexington ⟶ Braintree
Stoughton ⟶ Malden   Rockport ⟶ Wellesley
Boston ⟶ Lexington   Pembroke ⟶ Lawrence

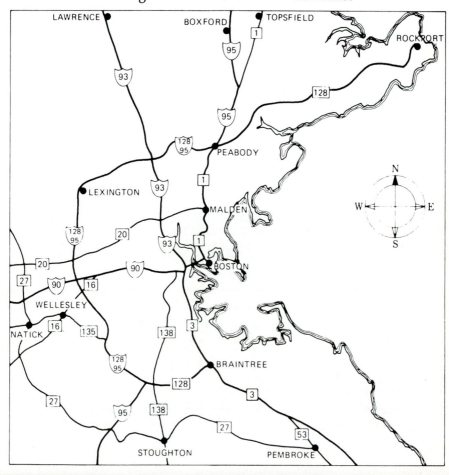

1 Introduce

1. **Read** (or play the tape for) the entire conversation. Explain the vocabulary, if necessary.
2. Model the names of places on the map and have students repeat in **chorus.**

2 Practice

1. **Read** (or play the tape for) the conversation again.
2. Practice parts of the conversation **T-S, S-S.**
3. **Pairwork.** Students practice asking for and giving directions. Call on pairs to role play for the class.
4. Check understanding by asking for the directions from different students. Work **T-S.** Encourage students to use gestures as they give and receive the information. Also, tell students it is a good idea to try to repeat directions to make sure they have heard them correctly.

3 Follow Up

1. Have students do **Workbook** page 48.
2. Tell students to imagine that they have a friend visiting from out of town. Their friend plans to rent a car at the airport and drive to their house, or take a taxi. Write directions to send to their friend. These directions should include written instructions and perhaps a map.

A. Write the correct question.

1. _____ It is Mary's.

2. _____ They are Tom's.

3. _____ This car is Jack's.

4. _____ That bike is Jack's.

B. Circle the correct word.

This
1. That   rackets are very good.
These

Those
2. This   car is Mary Brown's.
These

Those
3. This   shoes are too small.
That

This
4. Those   house is too big.
These

C. Fill in the missing words.

1. I _____ tired so John is helping _____.

2. Fred _____ tired so John is helping _____.

3. Maria _____ tired so John is helping _____.

4. The boys _____ tired so John is helping _____.

5. We _____ tired so John is helping _____.

Review/Enrich

1. Call on volunteers to hold up an article or articles (1 book, several pencils, 1 sweater, etc.) Ask a student:
   - **T:** Whose (pencil) is that? (point)
   - **S1:** This is my (pencil).
   - **T:** (Point and ask the same student about another article.) Whose (sweater) is that?
   - **S1:** That's (Ben's) (sweater).

2. **Dictation**. Dictate the following sentences slowly, but only twice. Tell students to repeat the sentence silently: then write:
   - a. These women are thin.　　　b. That shirt is Tom's.
   - c. This garage is the Johnsons'.

3. Practice pronouns in the following manner:
   - **T:** This (that) is my book. Give it to her. (point)
   - **S1:** This is her (his) pen. Give it to me.
   - **S2:** Those are (my) pencils. Give them to him. You may prompt this exchange until students get the idea.

4. Now have students change the possessive nouns to possessive adjectives.
   - a. Bess's skirt is red. (Her skirt is red.)
   - b. Tom's father is Jack. (His father is Jack.)
   - c. Mother's aunt is Sally.
   - d. Mary's jacket is under the bed.
   - e. Juan's ice skates are on the table.
   - f. The Johnsons' dog is in the yard.

5. **Song.** Use the model teaching plan on page 279 to introduce the song "Georgia on my Mind." Words and activities for the song are on page 283.

More Communicative Practice

Many people, especially ESL students, need to spell their names for someone else. Have students say the alphabet going quickly in a chain around the class. Ask several students to go to the board; have them ask classmates *How do you spell your last name?* Students dictate the spelling of their names as students at the board write. The students at the board check the spelling, asking *Right?*: students reply *That's right.* or *No, it's . . . .* Then have students change roles.

Objectives

Communication
Inquiring/Reporting: *time—(minutes) past/to (hour)*; *where/when/who's + going*; *future intention; directions*
Identifying: *places*

Grammar
review present progressive forms
going/wearing in future sense with time expressions
going to (future sense) + verbs
time phrases *in the afternoon, tonight, this morning,* etc.
time structures 10:30 (*ten-thirty*), 10:45 (*ten forty-five*)

Vocabulary/Expressions   Data Bank

afternoon	going to	party	tomorrow	1st	first
aunt	groceries	passengers	tonight	2nd	second
bike	highway	pick up	uncle	3rd	third
buy	hospital	plane	visit	4th	fourth
concert	hurry	play	with	5th	fifth
cousin	leaving	public restrooms			
dance (n.)	mail	return	Are there any		
deposit	mall	see	. . . nearby?		
evening	money	sir	Can you tell me . . . ?		
flight	movies	some	Good afternoon.		
football game	museum	take	Is it far to the . . . ?		
gas	night	taxi	It's late (early).		
gas station	package	today			
get					

Introduce the Unit

1. Briefly talk about the pictures. Be sure students see that it is one story. Ask:
   How many people are there?
   Who's going somewhere? (Explain, if necessary.)
   How do you know?
   Is she in a hurry? (Explain.)
   How do you know?
2. **Read** (or play the tape for) the dialogue once.
3. **Choral work** with the dialogue. Return to this page later and have several pairs act out the dialogue.

1. What time is it?   It's ten-fifteen.

2. What time is it?   It's ten-thirty.

3. What time is it?   It's ten-twenty.

4. What time is it?   It's ten forty-five.

—Hurry, it's late.
—What time is it?
—It's **ten-twenty.**
—No, it isn't. It's only **nine-thirty.** It's early.

1.

2.

3.

4.

1 Introduce

Note: Students should have no difficulty determining that the pictures depict both *face* and *digital* clocks.

Review time structures from page 30 briefly. With the help of a clock face with moving hands or clocks you draw on the board, review and/or teach:

> It's ten-fifteen/ten-twenty/ten-thirty/ten-forty-five.
> It's quarter to/past . . . .

2 Practice

1. Work **T-C** with the questions and answers.
2. Explain, if necessary: *Hurry . . . , it's late*, and *it's early*.
3. **Read** (or play the tape for) the dialogue. Work **T-C**, **T-S**, **S-S** with the substitution items.
4. **Pairwork**.

3 Follow Up

1. Have students work in groups of three. Write events (the name of a popular TV program, *bus, train, plane, movie, English class, work, dinner, party,* etc.) on small pieces of paper or cards. A student picks up a card and asks another student a question beginning with *What time is . . . ?* The students may respond with a real time or make one up. Or s(he) may respond *I don't know.* and ask another student. Encourage students to add the appropriate time of day, that is, *in the morning, in the afternoon, in the evening.*
2. If you didn't teach the **Fast Track** in Unit 2 (page 30), go back to it now and review the time expressions.

1 Introduce

(Books closed) Introduce new vocabulary using the pictures in the book—morning, evening, afternoon, night, and midnight.

2 Practice

1. **Read** the questions and answers in **chorus**. Make sure students understand the meanings of all the time phrases.
2. **Pairwork**.
3. **Read** (or play the tape for) the dialogue. Work **T-C**, **T-S** with the substitution items. Encourage students to make their own substitutions for destination, times, and flight numbers.
4. **Pairwork**.

Predictable Problem. The prepositions used in the time phrases in this unit should be drilled carefully. Some students may become confused as they encounter *in the afternoon*, *in the morning*, *in the evening*, *in the night*, *at midnight*, *at noon*. The absence of the article *the* with *at* and its presence with *in* also poses a problem.

> I'm going at noon/night/midnight/ten o'clock.
> I'm going *in the* morning/evening/afternoon.

Follow the lesson plan in order to give your students enough practice on this.

3 Follow Up

1. Have students do **Workbook** page 49.
2. Assign an actual phone call to an airline or travel agent. Students can inquire about flights to *any* destination they like. Encourage them to take notes during the phone call, and then write a full dialogue which can be presented to the class. This may be too difficult for some students.

1. When are you leaving? In the morning.

2. When are they leaving? In the evening.

3. When is she leaving? In the afternoon.

4. When is he leaving? At noon.

5. When are we leaving? At midnight.

6. When am I leaving? At night.

—Good afternoon.
—Good afternoon, sir.
—When is your next flight to Mexico?
—Tomorrow at **seven.**
—Seven **in the morning,** or seven **in the evening?**
—**In the evening.** It's flight 602.
—Thank you.
—Thank you, sir. Good-bye.

   1.   9:00   **morning/night**

   2.   12:00   **noon/midnight**

   3.   5:00   **morning/afternoon**

Where's Peter going? What's he going to do there?		He's going to the bank. He's going to deposit some money.

1. Where's she going?

   What's she going to do there?

   She's going to the post office.
She's going to mail a package.

2. Where are you going?

   What are you going to do there?

   I'm going to the supermarket.
I'm going to buy groceries.

3. Where are you going?

   What are you going to do there?

   We're going to the train station.
We're going to take a train.

4. Where are they going?

   What are they going to do there?

   They're going to the bus station.
They're going to take a bus.

1 Introduce

(Books closed)
1. Tell a student, *Go to the door.* Say *S(he)'s going to the door.* Then ask *What's s(he) going to do?* and answer *She's going to open the door.*
2. Walk around the room telling what you're doing (*going to the desk, door, board,* etc.) and what you're going to do (*going to open a book, close the door, write on the board,* etc.).
3. Have individual students move around the room telling where they are going and what they are going to do. Have other students tell where the moving students are going. Write and ask *Where's s(he) going? What's s(he) going to do?*

2 Practice

1. **Read** (or play the tape for) the model in the box and have students repeat in **chorus**. Point out that the pictures show the place where Peter is going.
2. **Read** (or play the tape for) all the questions and answers on pages 100 and 101. Do the following work with the *first* question and answer for each number.
3. **Pairwork.**
4. Check comprehension:
    T: Number 2. Is she going to the bank?
    S: No, she's going to the supermarket.
    T: Number 7. Is he going to the bus station?
    S: No, he's going to the theater. (etc.)

3 Follow Up

If students are progressing well, have them work with the text answers covered.

1   Introduce

The structure *going to* takes on a new meaning in the second question and answer for each number on pages 100 and 101. It is used to describe action that will take place in the future. Information questions are used to ask about what someone *is going to do* in the future—related to *where s(he) is going* at the moment. You may want to explain and use words like *now, soon, in a few minutes,* and *later* to help students understand the implied time.

2   Practice

1. **Read** (or play the tape for) the model in the box and have students repeat in **chorus**.
2. **Read** (or play the tape for) all the questions and answers on pages 100 and 101. Do the following work with the *second* question and answer for each number.
3. **Pairwork**
4. Check comprehension
   - **T**: Number 1. Is she going to take a train?
   - **S**: No, she's going to mail a package.
   - **T**: Number 5. Are they going to buy groceries?
   - **S**: No, they're going to visit a friend. (etc.)

3   Follow Up

1. Have students do **Workbook** page 50.
2. Quite a few new vocabulary words are presented on pages 100 and 101. Write the new words on small pieces of paper or cards. Have students pick a word and make a sentence or a question with it. Make a note of the words that seem to cause problems—and repeat the activity in a few days with these difficult words and any others from the unit.

5. Where are they going?

They're going to the hospital.

Why are they going there?

They're going to visit a friend.

6. Where's the taxi going?

It's going to the airport.

Why is it going there?

It's going to pick up passengers.

7. Where's he going?

He's going to the theater.

Why is he going there?

He's going to see a play.

8. Where's she going?

She's going to the library.

Why is she going there?

She's going to return some books.

9. Where are they going?

They're going to the gas station.

Why are they going there?

They're going to get gas.

ONE HUNDRED ONE/*Unit 9*/101

—Where are you going?
—I'm going to **London**.
—Who's going with you?
—**My mother** is.
—When are you going?
—**At ten o'clock.**

1. Rio   my cousin

2. New York City   my grandfather

3. Montreal   my grandmother

4. Mexico City   my aunt

5. Los Angeles   my uncle

1 Introduce

(Books closed) Ask students to give you the name of a city, a relative, and a time and write them on the board. Ask yourself questions in the following manner. Let students join in whenever they can:

> **T:** Are you going to Chicago?
> No, I'm not.
> Are you going to San Francisco?
> No, I'm not.
> Where are you going?
> (Point to destination on the board.) I'm going to New York.

> **T:** Is your brother going with you?
> No, he's not.
> Is your sister going with you?
> No, she's not.
> Who's going with you?
> (Point to the relative on the board.) My father is.

> **T:** Are you going at 7:30? (etc.)

Make sure that students understand the prepositions *to, with,* and *at.*

2 Practice

1. **Read** (or play the tape for) the model dialogue. Explain any new vocabulary. Have several pairs of students practice the dialogue and substitute the first two or three examples.
2. **Pairwork**.

3 Follow Up

In a few days, ask various students to act out this scene. They don't have to say exactly what's in the text. They will probably change the details, but their dialogues should run along the same line as the one on this page. If students have trouble remembering the questions in the dialogue, cue them with the question words *where, who,* and *when*?

1 Introduce

Write *TODAY* and then in a column underneath *this morning, this afternoon, this evening, tonight; TOMORROW* and then in a column underneath *tomorrow morning, tomorrow afternoon, tomorrow evening, tomorrow night.* Ask a student *When are you going?* and point to a time phrase. Student answers *I'm going . . . .*

2 Practice

1. **Read** (or play the tape for) the model dialogue. Have several pairs of students practice the dialogue and substitute the first two or three examples. Explain any new vocabulary.
2. **Pairwork**.

3 Follow Up

1. Have students do **Workbook** pages 51 and 52.
2. Ask the following or similar questions and have students write both the question and the answer. Be sure students realize there are no "wrong answers," as long as the answer is contextually correct in relation to the question.

    Where are you going tonight?
    What are you wearing?
    Who's going with you?
    When are you going?
    What are you going to do?

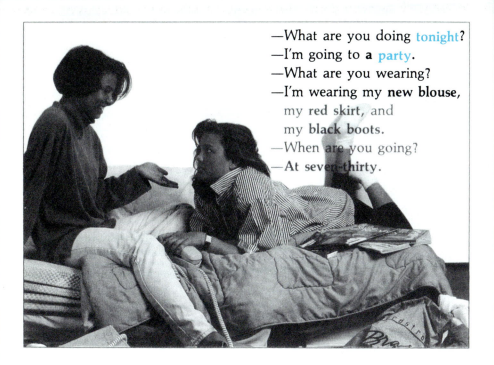

—What are you doing tonight?
—I'm going to **a** party.
—What are you wearing?
—I'm wearing my **new blouse**,
  my **red skirt**, and
  my **black boots**.
—When are you going?
—At seven-thirty.

1. tonight
   a dance
   blue dress, yellow scarf
   8:00

2. today
   the movies
   old jeans, white sweater
   4:30

3. **this morning**
   church
   brown coat, red hat
   6:30

4. **this afternoon**
   the football game
   yellow suit, brown shoes
   2:15

5. **tomorrow night**
   a concert
   black dress, white coat
   7:30

6. **Saturday night**
   the museum
   new slacks, gray blouse,
   green jacket
   8:15

ONE HUNDRED THREE/*Unit 9*/103

Role Play

1. Excuse me. Where's the post office?

   Go straight up the street. It's on the left.

2. Are there any public restrooms nearby?

   Yes, there are. Take your first right and then a left.

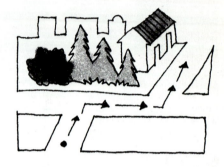

3. Is it far to the library?

   Well, take your first right on Main Street, then take your second left on School Street. It's right there.

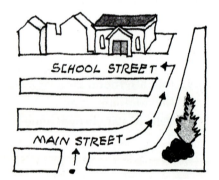

4. Can you tell me where Mike's Bike Store is?

   Mike's? Sure. Take the highway to Exit 12. It's in the new mall. You can't miss it.

Data Bank

1st	first	3rd	third	5th	fifth
2nd	second	4th	fourth		

1 Introduce

(Books closed) Write *straight, left, right, go, turn* on the board and explain.
Then have a student stand up and follow your directions around the classroom.
For example, you can say *Go straight ahead* and *Turn left at the second desk.*
Repeat with another student. Then have students give each other directions.
Use gestures if students are having trouble understanding.

2 Practice

1. **Read** (or play the tape for) the first conversation. Explain the vocabulary, if
   necessary
2. Work **T-C** with the conversation; switch roles.
3. Continue **T-S, S-S.**
4. Repeat with the other three conversations.

3 Follow Up

Have students work in groups of three or four to write directions to several
places in the general area of your classroom (administration office, restrooms,
parking lot, telephone, etc.) They should not write the destination with their
directions. If time allows, groups exchange directions. Students can either
figure out where the directions lead *or* they can actually follow the directions to
find the destination.

1 Introduce

1. Give students a minute to look over the map. Point to the places one at a time. Model the words and have students repeat.
2. **Read** the exercise at the bottom of the page. Do several examples, substituting different ways to ask for and give the same directions.

2 Practice

1. Work **T-C, T-S, S-S**.
2. **Pairwork.** Students practice asking for and giving directions. Call on pairs to role play for the class.
3. Check understanding by asking for the directions from different students. Work **T-S.** Encourage students to use gestures as they give and receive the information. Also, tell students it is a good idea to try to repeat directions to make sure they have heard them correctly.

3 Follow Up

Make a very simple map on the board of your downtown area; include some familiar stores or restaurants. Together figure out directions to and from different places. Have students repeat each time. Add a few more places to the map of the board and continue.

Work with your partner. Take turns asking for directions and giving directions "to" and "from."

1. From the hotel to the bookstore.
2. From the Post Office to the bus stop.
3. From the pharmacy to the bank.
4. From the bus stop to the Police Station.
5. From the school to the museum.
6. From the bridge to the school.
7. From the florist to the park.
8. From the beach to the hotel.

ONE HUNDRED FIVE/*Unit 9*/105

Pronunciation

I. | tall | teacher | ten | suit |
    |------|---------|-----|------|
    | to | eight | tonight | meat |
    | cemetery | water | student | pilot |

II. | building | bed | husband | bedroom |
    |----------|-----|---------|---------|
    | dancing | daughter | drinking | old |
    | dress | child | lemonade | blonde |

Her daughter is drinking lemonade.
Don is very handsome.

III. | thin | theater | three | throat |
     |------|---------|-------|--------|
     | thirty | tooth | thanks | thumb |

My tooth hurts *and* my throat hurts.
We're going to the theater at three-thirty.

IV. | that | these | other |
    |------|-------|-------|
    | father | there | brother |
    | mother | they | them |

That's my brother over there.
My mother's father is my grandfather.

V. That's Tom's lemonade.
    My father is a teacher.
    Tom's going to the theater with his brother tonight.
    They are both drinking tea.
    They're going to London at two-thirty.

1 Introduce

This page gives practice with the sounds of initial/final consonants *t* and *d* as well as the voiced and unvoiced sounds of *th*. Use the words *thin* and *that* to contrast the two sounds of *th*. There is a subtle difference here, so do not get too involved in isolating the *th's*.

2 Practice

Present in the usual way: students listening with books closed, **choral work**, **T-S**, **S-S**.

Predictable Problems. Some students may need extra practice with *d* in the final position; they may try to pronounce it as a soft *th* sound. Here are some extra words to add to those on the list you already have on page 106: *friend, glad, good, pleased, side, bread, bad, cold, around, tried, year, hundred*. Be sure students do not place their tongues between their teeth for the final *d* sound.

Some students may need extra practice with the voices *th* in the initial position as in *that*. First practice words in which the soft *th* sound occurs in the middle after a vowel: *father, mother, brother, other*, where the students may have more success with the sound. Once they know they can form the sound in one position, you may begin practice on the other more difficult one.

3 Follow Up

Have students use words from the page in sentences. They can read their sentences to a partner or to the class. Tell students to listen carefully for the sounds presented on the page.

1   Introduce

Explain carefully what students are to do: listen and write, on a separate piece of paper, the letter of the picture that best fits the dialogue.

2   Practice

1. **Read** (or play the tape for) the following:

Number 1
—Hurry, Sam. It's late.
—What time is it?
—It's ten-thirty.
—No, it isn't. It's only nine-twenty.

Answers
1. a, 2. b, 3. c, 4. a, 5. a

Number 2
—Where are you going?   —To Mexico.
—When is your plane?   —At seven-forty.
—Have a good time.   —Thank you.

Number 3
—Where are you going?   —To London.
—Who's going with you?   —My grandmother.
—When is your flight?   —At ten-fifteen.

Number 4
—What are you doing tonight?
—I'm going to a party.
—What are you wearing?
—My red skirt.
—When is the party?
—At nine.

Number 5
—When is the next plane to Mexico City?
—At midnight. It's flight 602.
—Thank you.

2. **Read** all five items again, pausing briefly for all students to re-examine their answers.

3   Follow Up

Have students do **Workbook** page 53.

Listen & Understand

Fast Track

—Hi! What's new?

—There's a new student in my English class. **He's** from **Brazil.**

—Oh, what does **he** look like?

—**He's tall and thin. He has black hair and wears glasses.**

—Tell me more.

—**He's friendly but quiet.**

Now make conversations with your partner.

pleasant	rude	short	red ⎫
hard-working	charming	fat	brown ⎬ hair
kind	loud	slim	black ⎭
shy	outgoing	husky	blue ⎫
serious	attractive	overweight	brown ⎬ eyes
unfriendly	unpleasant	skinny	
			has a ⎰ beard
			⎱ mustache

Mexico	Singapore
Germany	Costa Rica
Japan	Spain
Korea	Saudi Arabia
Colombia	Taiwan

108/*Unit 9*/ONE HUNDRED EIGHT

1 Introduce

1. **Read** (or play the tape for) the entire conversation. Explain the vocabulary, if necessary.
2. Review the difference between *What's s(he) like?* and *What does s(he) look like?* Tell the students to pretend they have a brother/sister and alternate asking them about what s(he)'s like and what s(he) looks like. Tell them to choose an adjective from the bottom of the page.

2 Practice

1. **Read** (or play the tape for) the conversation again.
2. Practice parts of the conversation **T-S, S-S.**
3. **Pairwork.** Have students work with the entire conversation.
4. Do **pairwork** with the substitution items. Students can practice and then role play in front of the class. This is a conversation which really does not need to be reproduced exactly. Students should be able to remember the general lines of the conversation and extend it easily.

3 Follow Up

1. Have students do **Workbook** page 54.
2. **Writing.** Have students write a paragraph about someone they know., a family member or a friend. Their paragraph should answer these questions:
   Where is this person from?
   What does this person look like?
   What is this person like?
   Do you like this person? Why or why not?
   Are you similar to or different from this person? In what ways?

A. Follow the model.

10:10   It's ten-ten._____

It's ten past ten._____

1. 11:15   _____

2. 12:30   _____

3. 1:45   _____

B. Answer the questions.

1. What's she going to do at the post office?

_____

2. What are they going to do at the train station?

_____

3. What are you going to do at the bank?

_____

4. What are you two going to do at the hospital?

_____

5. What's Mike going to do at the library?

_____

C. Write the questions.

1. _____ I'm going to London.

2. _____ My father is.

3. _____ At ten o'clock.

Review/Enrich

1. Have students write sentences using the following information. You may want to work the first ones with the class. This will be a challenge, but with help, students should be able to create their own sentences. Any correct sentence using all the information is acceptable:

    Montreal/9:30/my aunt
    (*I'm going to Montreal at 9:30. My aunt is going with me.*)
    library/5:30/return a book   museum/tonight/Jim
    football game/tomorrow/Ted   party/this afternoon/red dress, (etc.)

2. Have students list as many place names as they can think of. List on the board. Pretend that you are having trouble writing the words and ask students *How do you spell that?* Then have students put all the words in alphabetical order.

3. Say the following sentences, one at a time. Have students write or say the corresponding questions for each sentence. Tell students that they can form two questions from each sentence. If they have trouble getting started, give them the question words (shown in parentheses).

    Bill is wearing a green shirt. (What, Who)
    The dog is under the table. (What, Where)
    My grandmother is behind the sofa. (Who, Where)
    She's going to the library at eight o'clock. (When, Where)
    The next bus is at five o'clock. (What, When)

More Communicative Practice

Have students work in groups of three or four. Tell them to create a weekend sightseeing plan for a group of tourists visiting a city they are familiar with. The plan should include activities for Saturday and Sunday—morning, afternoon, and evening. Write a sample entry on the board:

    Saturday morning
    9:00 Central Park—see the lake and the zoo
    10:30 Museum of Modern Art—visit modern paintings exhibit (etc.)

Then have groups in turn write their sightseeing plan on the board or on a large "poster" so everyone in the class can see it. Have other students ask group members questions like:

    Where is/are . . . going at . . . ?
    Who's . . . going with . . . ?
    What is/are . . . going to do?

Since this could be rather an extensive project, you might want to assign it to one group per week and give students time to prepare outside class.

Objectives

Communication
Giving/Seeking/Denying:*permission*
Inquiring/Reporting: *ability/knowledge*; *calendar, vacation, weather, shows*
Identifying: *sports, games, skills*

Grammar
auxiliary verb: *can*
contraction: *can't*
verb: *have to* (*has to*)
prepositions of time *on, in, at*

Vocabulary/Expressions

				Data Bank
adults	drizzling	sing	warm	jazz
after	enjoy	sit	wash	soccer
be	fall (n.)	skate	weather	
before	grooming	ski	wet paint	
breakfast	hands	snowing	windows	
brush	have	spring	windy	
can	help	start	winter	
can't	hot	study	year	
change	looking	summer		
circus	lunch	sun	a lot	
clean	math	sunny	Are you sure . . . ?	
clothes	polish	taking	Come in.	
cloudy	pouring	tennis	Hurry up!	
cold	programmer	tickets	Oh dear.	
computer	raining	type	Right!	
dinner	read	use	See you soon.	
drinks	rock concert	vacation	Stop!	
drive	run	wait		
	school	walk		
	sign			

Introduce the Unit

Read (or play the tape for) this page as a preview of Unit 10. Make sure that students understand what a dog grooming school is. Ask yourself questions like *Can I type?* and *Can I drive a taxi?* Answer *Yes, I can* or *No, I can't*. Ask students the same questions.

Write *Yes, I am.* and *Yes, I'm sure.* on the board. Then ask students *Are you sure you can type?* (etc.)

10

Can Sally skate?  No, she can't.

1. Can Sam type?  No, he can't.

2. Can they ski?  Yes, they can.

3. Can they run?  Yes, they can.

4. Can it sing?  Yes, it can.

5. Can it sing? No, it can't.

6. Can you walk? No, we can't.

7. Can he drive?  No, he can't.

110/*Unit 10*/ONE HUNDRED TEN

1 Introduce

Ask a student to come to the front of the class and pantomime playing tennis.
Say to the rest of the class:

> Can s(he) play tennis?
>
> Yes, s(he) can./No, s(he) can't.

Repeat with several students pantomiming other activities. Now let students
ask and answer the questions.

2 Practice

1. **Read** (or play the tape for) the questions and answers in the usual manner.
   Note that the pictures give clues to the unfamiliar verbs on this page. The
   pictures also show that *can* is used here in the sense of *to be able to*.
2. **Pairwork**.

3 Follow up

1. Have students do **Workbook** page 55.
2. **Writing.** Write these questions on the board. Say to the students. *Here are
   the questions. Write only the answers.*

> a. Can you type?
>
> b. Can you sing?
>
> c. What can you play?

Write these answers on the board. Say, *Here are the answers. Write only
the answers.*

> d. Yes, I can.
>
> e. No, I can't.
>
> f. No, I'm sorry. I can't use a computer.

1 Introduce

(Books closed) Try to lift a heavy object or do some difficult task, and ask:

      T: Can you help me? (Explain.)
      S: Yes, I can./No, I can't.

Change roles and have a student pretend to be doing something difficult and ask if you can help him/her. Reply in the negative: *No, I can't. I have to help Mario.* Talk with another student; reply *No, I'm sorry. I have to wash the clothes.* Write both exchanges on the board.

2 Practice

1. **Read** (or play the tape) in the usual way.
2. **Pairwork**.

Predictable Problem. Students may try to use the *-ing* form of a verb after *can: He can playing soccer.* Some students may even try to say: *He can to play soccer.* Explain that the verb after *can/can't* never changes from its simple form.

3 Follow Up

1. Have students do **Workbook** page 56.
2. **Build Up the Board** in the following manner:

      T: I have a lot to do.
           Can . . . (Mary/Jack) help me? (Explain and write.)
           No, I'm sorry. S(he) has to study. (Explain and write.)
      S: Can . . . help me?
      T: No, I'm sorry. S(he) has to wash the clothes. (Explain and write.)
           Can . . . help me?
      T: No, I'm sorry. S(he) has to clean the windows/brush the dog/polish the car.

**I have a lot to do.
Can you help me?**

**No, I'm sorry.
I have to
wash the clothes.**

1. Mary has a lot
   to do.
   Can Tommy
   help her?

No, I'm sorry.
He has to study.

2. Jack has a lot
   to do.
   Can Susan
   help him?

No, I'm sorry.
She has to
clean the windows.

3. They have a lot
   to do.
   Can Bill
   help them?

No, I'm sorry.
He has to
brush the dog.

4. We have a lot
   to do.
   Can Fred and Ron
   help us?

No, I'm sorry.
They have to
polish the car.

5. Well, I'm going
   to play tennis.

No, you can't.
You have to
help *me*!

ONE HUNDRED ELEVEN/*Unit 10*/111

THE CONCERT

Jack is waiting for Gloria.
They're going to a rock concert.
The concert is at seven o'clock.
It's quarter to seven now.
But Gloria is late.
She's still at home.
She's washing her hair.

—Gloria, hurry up. We have
   to go. It's ten to seven now,
   and the concert is at seven.
—No, the concert is at eight.
   Look in the newspaper.
—I *am* looking in the
   newspaper. The concert is at
   seven. Can't you read?
—Oh dear. I'm sorry. Well,
   come in and wait.

—No, I can wait in the yard.
   I can sit here and...
—No! Stop! You can't sit...
—Oh yes I can.
—Oh Jack. Look at your pants.
   Look at your hands!
   Look at the sign! Can't *you*
   read?
—Oh. Wet Paint.
   Well, don't hurry, Gloria.
   I have to go home and
   change my suit.

1 Introduce

Use the guessing game technique to introduce this page. Tell the class that two people are going somewhere. Have students write their guesses to the following questions. You write some "wrong" guesses on the board.

Is the boy's name Jack or Tony?
Is the girl's name Gloria?
Are they going to the movies or to a rock concert?

2 Practice

1. **Read** (or play the tape for) the entire page through without stopping. Discuss the students' guesses and put all the correct answers on the board. Ask *Right or Wrong?* with these:

The concert is at seven.
Jack is looking at the newspaper.
Gloria is still at the library.
She's reading a book.
Jack has to go home and wash his hair.

2. **Read** the page again with students repeating in **chorus**.
3. **Pairwork** with the dialogue.

3 Follow Up

Culture Capsule. Jack and Gloria are going on a "date." They may or may not be meeting a group of friends at the concert, and they are not taking along a *chaperone*. Jack will probably provide the transportation and pay all expenses, although they may go "dutch," that is, Jack will pay half and Gloria will pay half. How does this situation compare with a typical date in your culture?

Asking for a date is usually the most difficult part of the process. Ask the unmarried students what they usually say to ask someone out. Ask them how they feel when they ask someone out (scared, happy, nervous). Ask students who usually pays or if they go dutch. Ask everyone where they like to go— when they are on a date or with a group of friends.

1 Introduce

1. Write the days of the week on the board and practice in **chorus**.
    Ask: *Where are you going on Sunday?* As the students reply, write the
    answers under the appropriate day of the week.

    > **T**: Where are you going on Sunday?
    >
    > **S**: I'm going swimming on Sunday. (Write: swimming on Sunday.)
    > (Underline _on_.)

    Continue with *When* questions: *When are you going swimming?* etc.
2. Quickly present *before* and *after*. Point to Monday and say:

    > Monday is before Tuesday and after Sunday.
    > What is before Friday? Saturday? Sunday?
    > What's after Monday? Tuesday? (etc.)
3. Write the names of the months on the board and work in **chorus**. Write
    your name under one month and names of students under the rest. Explain
    new vocabulary as you go along. Underline _in_.

    > I'm taking my vacation in January. (Write _in_ January.)
    > When are you taking your vacation this year? (_In_ . . .)
    > When is . . . (Joe) taking his vacation this year? (Refer to board.)

2 Practice

1. **Read** (or play the tape for) the first dialogue. Work **T-C**, **T-S**, **S-S** with the
    substitution items.
2. **Pairwork**. Listen for the preposition *on* in students' answers.
3. Repeat for the second dialogue.
4. **Pairwork**. Listen for the preposition *in* in students' answers.

3 Follow Up

1. Have students do **Workbook** page 57.
2. Prepare two sets of cards: one with the names of the months, the other with
    activities and sports (*read a book, play tennis, use a computer,* etc.). Put
    the cards face down on a desk and ask a student to pick a card from each
    pile. Then have the student ask a question with *can,* for example, *Can you
    play tennis in January?* Explain that asking the question this way with *you*
    is a way of asking the general question *Is it possible to play tennis in
    January?* This may also be done in **pairs** or small groups.

Culture Capsule. The seasons shown here are according to the *North American* climate. Compare and contrast the months and seasons to your own
environment. Yours may be identical, similar, or completely opposite. The local
environment may have *dry* and *rainy* seasons as well.

—When are the **Smiths** coming for dinner?
—On **Sunday.**

1.

2.

3.

4.

5.

6.

—When are you taking your vacation this year?
—In **January.**
—Oh, do you like a winter vacation?
—Yes.

WINTER	January
	S M T W T F S
	    1 2 3 4 5 6
	7 8 9 10 11 12 13
	14 15 16 17 18 19 20
	21 22 23 24 25 26 27
	28 29 30 31
		WINTER	February
			S M T W T F S
			           1 2 3
			4 5 6 7 8 9 10
			11 12 13 14 15 16 17
			18 19 20 21 22 23 24
			25 26 27 28
				SPRING	March
					S M T W T F S
					           1 2 3
					4 5 6 7 8 9 10
					11 12 13 14 15 16 17
					18 19 20 21 22 23 24
					25 26 27 28 29 30 31

SPRING	April
	S M T W T F S
	1 2 3 4 5 6 7
	8 9 10 11 12 13 14
	15 16 17 18 19 20 21
	22 23 24 25 26 27 28
	29 30
		SPRING	May
			S M T W T F S
			      1 2 3 4 5
			6 7 8 9 10 11 12
			13 14 15 16 17 18 19
			20 21 22 23 24 25 26
			27 28 29 30 31
				SUMMER	June
					S M T W T F S
					              1 2
					3 4 5 6 7 8 9
					10 11 12 13 14 15 16
					17 18 19 20 21 22 23
					24 25 26 27 28 29 30

SUMMER	July
	S M T W T F S
	1 2 3 4 5 6 7
	8 9 10 11 12 13 14
	15 16 17 18 19 20 21
	22 23 24 25 26 27 28
	29 30 31
		SUMMER	August
			S M T W T F S
			        1 2 3 4
			5 6 7 8 9 10 11
			12 13 14 15 16 17 18
			19 20 21 22 23 24 25
			26 27 28 29 30 31
				FALL	September
					S M T W T F S
					                1
					2 3 4 5 6 7 8
					9 10 11 12 13 14 15
					16 17 18 19 20 21 22
					23 24 25 26 27 28 29
					30

FALL	October
	S M T W T F S
	    1 2 3 4 5 6
	7 8 9 10 11 12 13
	14 15 16 17 18 19 20
	21 22 23 24 25 26 27
	28 29 30 31
		FALL	November
			S M T W T F S
			           1 2 3
			4 5 6 7 8 9 10
			11 12 13 14 15 16 17
			18 19 20 21 22 23 24
			25 26 27 28 29 30
				WINTER	December
					S M T W T F S
					                1
					2 3 4 5 6 7 8
					9 10 11 12 13 14 15
					16 17 18 19 20 21 22
					23 24 25 26 27 28 29
					30 31

ONE HUNDRED THIRTEEN/*Unit 10*/113

1. What's the weather like?   It's drizzling.

2. What's the weather like?   It's raining.

3. What's the weather like?   It's pouring.

4. What's the weather like?   It's snowing.

5. What's the weather like?   It's hot.

6. What's the weather like?   It's warm.

7. What's the weather like?   It's cold.

8. What's the weather like?   It's cloudy.

9. What's the weather like?   It's sunny.

10. What's the weather like?   It's windy.

114/*Unit 10*/ONE HUNDRED FOURTEEN

1 Introduce

Note: *It is* and *It's* are used as sentence starters in statements about time and weather.

Establish the meaning of *weather*. Use the pictures in the text to explain the weather vocabulary. Write the words on the board. Ask:
Is it hot or cold? Is it raining or snowing?
Is it cloudy? Is it windy?
What's the weather like?

2 Practice

1. **Read** (or play the tape for) the questions and answers.
2. Have students work in **pairs** in the usual manner. Be sure that they exchange roles and then cover the type and use only the pictures in forming the correct weather expressions.

Predictable Problem. Some students may become confused between the *-ing* forms (*It's raining.*) and the adjective forms (*It's hot.*) The result may be something like *It's rain* (incorrect). Listen very carefully and be sure that you hear the final *-ing* in *drizzling, raining, pouring, snowing.* Insist on its presence, but do not overemphasize this unaccented syllable.

3 Follow Up

1. Have students do **Workbook** page 58.
2. Come back to this page at the end of the unit as a review of the months and the weather. Work in the following manner:
T: January
S1: What's the weather like in January?
S2: It's . . . . (etc.)

1   Introduce

Review terms for weather by asking students *What's the weather like in . . .*
(substitute the four seasons)*?* with reference to the local weather.

2   Practice

(Books closed for Step 1.)
1. **Read** (or play the tape for) the first dialogue. Then ask:
    Where is John?
    What's the weather like in San Francisco?
    When is John leaving San Francisco?
    What's the weather where his friend is?
  Have students open their books to page 115.
2. **Read** the dialogue again as students follow silently.
3. **Read** (or play the tape for) the second dialogue.

3   Follow Up

Point out that students may substitute freely in these two exercises. Pay
special attention to individual performances as you monitor the **pairwork**, and
use as a check of students' abilities to use the language independently.

—Hi, this is **John** in **San Francisco**.
—Hi, **John**.
When are you coming?
—I'm leaving here at **nine** o'clock.
What's the weather like there?
—It's hot and sunny here.
What's the weather like in
San Francisco?
—It's **raining**.
—Well, come and enjoy the sun.
—Right! See you soon.

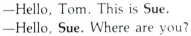

—Hello, Tom. This is **Sue**.
—Hello, **Sue**. Where are you?
—I'm on vacation in **Florida**.
—What's the weather like?
—It's **hot**.

ONE HUNDRED FIFTEEN/*Unit 10*/115

Role Play

Good morning. Can I help you?

Yes, thanks. I'd like tickets to the circus.

Which day?

Monday.

The afternoon or evening show?

What time does the afternoon show start?

It starts at 3:30.

That's fine. Two children and two adults, please.

That's $28.00, please.

Here you are.

And here's your change. Enjoy the show.

Thank you.

Data Bank

JAZZ
FEBRUARY 12
$18 $15

HAMLET
SEPT 20 - 2:00
$20 $15

DANCE
MARCH 2 300-
$25 $20

SOCCER
JUNE 19 1:30
$10

1 Introduce

1. Ask students where this conversation takes place (at a ticket office, an auditorium, or other place where people usually buy tickets).
2. **Read** (or play the tape for) the conversation.
3. Ask students the following questions to check understanding:
   > What does she want tickets for? (the circus)
   > What day does she want to go to the circus? (Monday)
   > What time does the afternoon show start? (3:30)
   > How many tickets does she want? (four tickets)
   > How much are they? ($28.00)

2 Practice

1. **Read** (or play the tape for) the conversation again.
2. Work **T-C, T-S, S-S** as usual with pairs of lines from the conversation.
3. **Pairwork.** Have students practice buying and selling tickets substituting different information from the Data Bank posters. Have pairs present conversations for the class.

3 Follow Up

Writing. Have students write a paragraph about some type of entertainment they enjoy. They can include where and when it usually takes place and what they like about it.

1 Introduce

Have students read the conversations silently. Call on several **pairs** to make the conversations. If students have difficulty, remind them to look for the key words in every line that signal the correct sequence. for example, explain that you know you can not respond to *Can I help you?* with *Yes, a few* . . .; therefore choose *Yes, three tickets* . . . . Then let student finish figuring out the sequencing.

2 Practice

1. **Read** the conversations.
2. Work **T-C, T-S** with the conversations.
3. **Pairwork,** Have students practice the conversations. Encourage them to stand up and use gestures and props (small cards for tickets and paper for money).
4. **On Your Own.** Read the directions and the two situations. Ask simple comprehension questions to make sure they understand the situations.
5. **Pairwork.** Students make their own conversations with the situations.

3 Follow Up

Draw two posters on the board or have students make up additional situations. Encourage them to use situations based on real events they have attended or are happening in the area. Have students use the posters on the board or these additional situations to create their own dialogues.

Say the Right Thing!

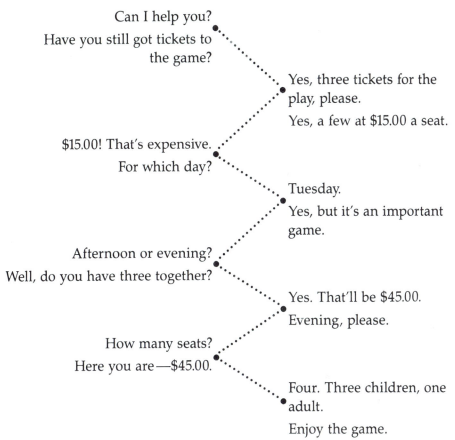

Can I help you?

Have you still got tickets to the game?

Yes, three tickets for the play, please.

Yes, a few at $15.00 a seat.

$15.00! That's expensive.

For which day?

Tuesday.

Yes, but it's an important game.

Afternoon or evening?

Well, do you have three together?

Yes. That'll be $45.00.

Evening, please.

How many seats?

Here you are—$45.00.

Four. Three children, one adult.

Enjoy the game.

On Your Own

Make conversations with your partner.

1. You want to go to the Whale Show.
   Buy tickets for two children and two adults.
   Buy the tickets for Wednesday night.

2. You want to go to the play.
   Buy tickets for one child and one adult.
   Buy the tickets for Saturday night.

Read and Enjoy

HOW I HELPED THE TRAVELER

Main Street? Yessir. Let me see—
If it isn't this street, it must be
The next or the next on the left or right.
Just go down here to the traffic light
And take a turn, or go straight ahead.
(You have to stop if the light is red.)
—That could be Main. If it's not Main,
Go round the block and try again.
You just can't miss it. It's in plain sight:
Straight ahead, or left, or right.

John Ciardi

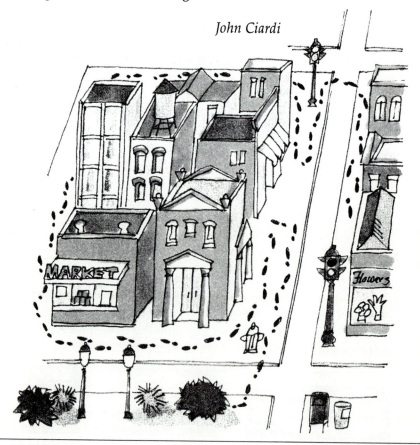

118/*Unit 10*/ONE HUNDRED EIGHTEEN

1   Introduce

Read (or play the tape for) the poem. Explain anything that students do not understand. Ask them why they think the poet put the words *Yes* and *sir* together to make one word *Yessir* (because people *say* it that way). Ask them if they can find a phrase in the poem that means "right in front of you" (*in plain sight*). Students should be able to find a lot of rhyming words (*see/be, right/ light,* etc.).

2   Practice

1. Go through the poem **T-C.** The class can read the poem in **chorus.**
2. **Read** the poem line by line as you snap your fingers to the rhythm. Students repeat.
3. This poem has a musical rhythm. If there are students who like to perform, have them stand in a row—pretending they are standing with a group of buddies on a street corner. They can pretend to be giving someone directions and recite the poem in "relay," snapping their fingers and gesturing as they recite. Encourage them to imagine who this group of people are: men or women or both, teenage or older, etc.

3   Follow Up

This would be a good time to get students to compose their own poem by substituting in this poem. As long as the word you want to substitute has the same number of syllables, you will maintain the rhythm of the original. For example, substituting the word *First* for *Main* in the first and seventh lines would work. Of course, you might lose the rhyme, but the most important thing is to get students to play with the words. They might also be able to compose short poems with one or two rhyming pairs.

1 Introduce

Explain carefully what students are to do: listen and write, on a separate piece of paper, the letter of the picture that best fits the dialogue.

2 Practice

Read (or play the tape for) the following:

Number 1
—Good afternoon, Peter.
—Hello, Mrs. Park. Can Laura play with me?
—No, she can't. She has to wash the windows.
—Oh, can I help her?

Answers
1. a, 2. b, 3. b, 4. a, 5. a

Number 2
—Come on Jack. We're late for the concert.
—What time is it?
—It's ten to seven.
—But, the rock concert is at eight!
—No, it isn't. It's at seven.

Number 3
—Are you going on vacation this year?   —Yes, in July.
—Where are you going?   —To Florida.
—M-m-m. It's nice and hot there.

Number 4
—What's the weather like?   —I don't know.
—Well, look out of the window!   —B-r-r-r. It's cold.
—Cold?   —Yes. People are wearing hats and coats.
—Well, I'm glad it's not raining.

Number 5
—Hello, Peter. Where are you phoning from?
—California.
—What's the weather like?
—It's raining. What's the weather like in New York?
—Is it cold? Is it snowing?
—No, it's cloudy, but it's not raining.

3 Follow Up

Have students do **Workbook** page 59.

Listen & Understand

Fast Track

—Hello. **Downtown Theater**.
—Hello. What time is the **movie** today?
—There is a **movie three times a day, 11:00, 1:00, and 3:00.**
—Thank you very much. Bye!

Now make your own conversations with a partner.

- Captain Jack's
  Whale Watch

- Fantastic Trips
  Sightseeing Tours

- Harry's Ha Ha
  Comedy Show

- Elegant Fashion
  Show

every { hour
hour on the hour
hour on the half hour }

once
twice
three times } a day/an evening etc.

every { two
three hours, etc. }

1 Introduce

Bring in to class or have students bring in to class several copies of the entertainment section of a local newspaper. Pretend that you are trying to plan a class outing and you have to decide where to go, when, etc. Students will probably know a lot of the vocabulary they need for this discussion.

2 Practice

1. **Read** the conversation. The only expression you may have to explain is *three times a day,* meaning "three times each day." Then ask them how to say "two times each month" (you can give them the word *twice*) and "five times each year."
2. Practice parts of the conversation **T-S, S-S.**
3. **Pairwork.** Have students work with the entire conversation.
4. Do **pairwork** with the substitution items at the bottom of the page. Explain the expression *every hour on the . . .* (*hour* means at 4:00, 5:00, etc.; *half hour* means 4:00, 4:30, 5:00, 5:30, etc.).

3 Follow Up

1. Have students do **Workbook** page 60.
2. **Writing.** Have students write a radio script announcing a local event. They can work in **pairs** or in groups of three or four. Make sure they have included all the details (dates, times, place) and encourage them to promote the event, so they will attract a lot of people to buy tickets. They can **read** their advertisement to the rest of the class. Then ask the other students if they would like to attend the event and why or why not.

A. Circle the correct word.

1. A cat can
   type.
   ski.
   walk.

2. A pilot can
   polish.
   fly.
   sing.

3. A dog can
   run fast.
   study math.
   clean windows.

B. Circle the correct word.

1. You   have   to help me.
           has

2. Mary   have   to go now.
           has

3. I   have   to study.
           has

4. They   have   to wash the clothes.
           has

C. What's the weather like?

1. _____   2._____   3._____

D. Write the missing months.

January _____ March _____ May

_____ July _____ September

_____ November _____

Review/Enrich

1. To practice time prepositions *on*, *in*, and *at*, write the following or similar questions on the board. Students will write any correct short answers. They must use *on*, *in*, and *at* in their answers. Read the questions and allow students time to write their answers.

   When is your vacation?   When is your grandmother coming?
   When is your father going to the store? (etc.)

   Variation. Reverse the above procedure and write short answers on the board. Students will write appropriate questions.

   On Sunday.   In the fall.   In August
   At ten-thirty.   In the evening. (etc.)

2. Write familiar place names on the board or use pictures or photographs, and begin a question chain. Have students answer negatively:
   No, I can't. I have to . . . .

   T: Can you go to the movies? (Show a picture or write the word.)
   S1: No, I can't. I have to (help my father).
   (Show the next picture or write the word. Student 1 will continue.)
   S1: (to another student) Can you go to the . . . ? (picture or word)
   S2: No, I can't. I have to . . . .
       (to another student) Can you go to the . . . ? (picture or word)
   S3: No, ...(etc.)

   Variation. Repeat, but have students ask about someone else:
   Can s(he) go to . . . ?   Can they . . . ?
   Can s(he) go skating/swimming?

3. **Dictation**. Have students complete the following sentences with a prepositional phrase.
   a. The children have to eat dinner . . . (at one o'clock.)
   b. I like to take my vacation . . . .   d. He can't come to dinner . . . .
   c. The party is . . . .   e. The next bus is . . . .

4. **Song.** Use the model teaching plan on page 279 to introduce the song "Mail Myself to You." Words and activities for the song are on page 284.

More Communicative Practice

Have each student pretend to be planning a vacation. Write the following questions on the board as a guide:

   Where are you going?   When are you going?
   Who's going with you?   What are you wearing?

The following test will give you a fair idea of what students know after completing Book 1. We offer this test as a guide only, and you may adapt it according to the needs of your own students. However, we encourage you to evaluate in some fashion upon completion of the book, especially in the areas of listening and speaking. You may want to give your test over a two-day period, dividing the sections where appropriate.

NOTE: Reproduce the student answer sheets provided on pages 277 and 278 or have students answer on a separate piece of paper.

I. Listening

A. Dictate the following sentences. Each sentence is worth four points.

1. Is her name Mary?
2. Sally is wearing a green sweater.
3. The jacket is under the table.
4. What color is her hair?
5. Where's he sitting?
6. My sister is a secretary, and so is my cousin.
7. There are two cars in the garage.
8. Dick can clean the house for us.
9. Who's going to the theater with you?
10. Sue and Tom aren't in the yard.

B. Return to page 95 and read the following dialogues. Students are to listen and write the letter of the picture that best fits the dialogue they hear. Each answer is worth two points.

1. - Where's your brother?
   - He's in the yard.
   - What's he doing?
   - He's washing the car.
   - Is your sister helping him?
   - No, she isn't.

2. - Is this Tom's new jacket?
   - No, it isn't. His new jacket is blue. That jacket is green.

3. - Are these your new boots?
   - Yes, they are.

4. - That's a nice blue house.
    - Yes. Whose is it?
    - It's the Brown's house.
    - Is that their car, too?
    - No, that's my car.

5. - Where are the children?
    - They're in the garage.
    - What are they doing?
    - They're cleaning it.
    - Is the dog helping them?
    - No, it isn't.

Answers: 1. c   2. c   3. a   4. a   5. b

II. Speaking

Allow time to thoroughly practice the three sample dialogues with your students. You may write the sample dialogues on the board to help students complete the sentences. Then have student pairs take ten minutes to choose one of the sample conversations and create a similar dialogue. Walk around checking and encouraging pairs. After ten minutes, have each pair present its dialogue in front of the class. Use your judgment as to how many points (20 possible) each dialogue is worth.

1. What's your name?	My name is . . . (student's name)
Is your name . . .?	Yes, it is. No, it isn't.
What's your last name?	It's . . . . (student's last name)
How old are you?	I'm . . . (student's age)
Are you a . . . (teacher)?	Yes, I am. No, I'm a . . . (student)
Are you . . . (Mexican)?	Yes, I am. No, I'm . . . (Japanese)
2. What are you doing?	I'm . . . (reading, watching, etc.)
Where are you going?	I'm going to . . . (the movies, etc.)
When are you going?	At . . . (four, two-thirty, etc.)

3. Is that your . . . (hat)?   Yes, it is.
                                                  No, it isn't.

    What color is your . . . (coat)?   It's . . . (color)

    Is . . . (student's name)   No, s(he's) wearing a . . .
    wearing a . . . (skirt)?

III. Reading/Writing

A.   Have students select the best answers in this section. Each answer is worth one point.

                1. b   2. a   3. b   4. c   5. c

B.   Have students read the story and answer the questions. Each correct answer is worth two points.

1.   Bob is in the living room.
2.   He is reading the newspaper.
3.   He can play the piano.
4.   The dog is eating Bob's slippers.
5.   Bob is Canadian.

C.   Have students write a brief story about themselves. Accept any reasonable statements. This paragraph is worth fifteen points.

I. Listening

A. Write the sentences you hear.

1. _____
2. _____
3. _____
4. _____
5. _____
6. _____
7. _____
8. _____
9. _____
10. _____

B. What's the best answer?

1. _____
2. _____
3. _____
4. _____
5. _____

II. Speaking

Your teacher will give you directions for this exercise.

III. Reading/Writing

A. Choose the best answer.

Example: Hello, Judy.
    a. Yes, she is.
    b. Hi.
    c. No, I'm not.
    d. It's Fred.

1. How old are you?
    a. I'm fine.
    b. I'm sixteen.
    c. No, I'm not.
    d. At ten o'clock.

2. Anything else?

a. That's all, thank you.
b. Very well, thank you.
c. Yes, I am, thank you.
d. Yes, it is, thank you.

3. What time is it?

a. It's Mary.
b. It's seven o'clock.
c. At seven o'clock.
d. At the bus stop.

4. This is my friend Tom.

a. Tom is.
b. No, he isn't.
c. Glad to meet you, Tom.
d. So long, Tom.

5. She can't do it alone.

That's okay. John can help . . .
a. them
b. him
c. her
d. she

B. Read the following story and answer the questions.

Bob is Canadian. He can play the piano. He is reading the newspaper in his living room. His dog is eating his slippers!

1. Where is Bob? _____

2. What is he doing? _____

3. Can he play the flute or the piano? _____

4. Who's eating Bob's slippers? _____

5. What is Bob's nationality? _____

C. Write a story about yourself like the one about Bob.

_____

_____

_____

_____

_____

_____

1 Introduce the Songs

1. (First song only) Write the words *verse* and *chorus* on the board. Explain that songs have a number of verses (first, second, third, etc.) and a chorus that is repeated between verses.
2. Make copies of the songs and distribute these song sheets to students. Write the name of the song and any unfamiliar words on the board. Model the words and have students repeat them in chorus.
3. **Colors.** Tell the students that this is a love song. Although the song was written by a Scottish folk singer in the 1960's, it became popular in the U.S. and was recorded by many others.
   Give My Regards to Broadway. This song about the theater district of New York City has been popular for a long time. Visitors to the city still line up to see plays and musicals on Broadway.
   This Land is Your Land. Woody Guthrie traveled around the country singing and writing songs about the places he saw. This song celebrates the beauty of the land and the ideals of its people.
   Georgia on my Mind. In this beautiful song, the singer compares his love to a song that he can't get out of his mind. It is associated with the popular singer Ray Charles.
   Mail Myself to You. This nonsense song shows a more humorous side of Woody Guthrie. People of all ages have enjoyed singing it.

2 Practice the Songs

1. Play the tape for the song several times. Discuss parts of the song and verify that students have understood.
2. Encourage students to sing along with the tape.
3. Ask students if they like the song; discuss why or why not.

3 Follow Up

1. Have students do the exercises at the bottom of the song sheet.
2. You can come back to the songs later as a break from other practice. Or when you introduce a new song, ask students if they want to listen to or sing one of the songs they have already learned.
3. If you have students who sing or play an instrument, they may be able to learn the song and perform it for the class.
4. Whenever possible, encourage students to create additional verses of their own, or to replace key words in the song to reflect their own lives and experiences.

Colors

by Donovan

1. Yellow is the color of my true love's hair
   In the morning, when we rise,
   In the morning, when we rise.
   That's the time, that's the time, I love the best.

2. Blue is the color of the sky
   In the morning, when we rise,
   In the morning, when we rise,
   That's the time, that's the time, I love the best.

3. Green's the color of the sparklin' corn
   In the morning, when we rise,
   In the morning, when we rise,
   That's the time, that's the time, I love the best.

A. Fill in the missing words.

1. Three colors in the song are _____,
   _____, and _____.
2. My favorite color is _____.
3. Corn is good to _____.

B. Write out the contraction.

That's = _____ + _____

C. Answer the questions.

1. What color is your hair?

   _____

2. What time of day is the best in the song?

   _____

3. What is your favorite time of day?

   _____

Give My Regards to Broadway

by George Cohan

1. Give my regards to Broadway,
   remember me to Herald Square.
   Tell all the gang at Forty Second Street
   that I will soon be there.

2. Tell them of how I'm yearning
   to mingle with the oldtime throng.
   Give my regards to old Broadway and tell them
   I'll be there ere long.

A. Find words in the song.

1. Say hello to (first verse) = _____

2. A small group of friends are a _____. (first verse)

3. A large group of people are a _____. (second verse)

B. Write out the contraction.

I'm = _____ + _____

I'll = _____ + _____

C. What words rhyme?

In the first verse, _____ and _____ rhyme.

In the second verse, _____ and _____ rhyme.

D. Answer the questions.

1. What is the name of a street in the song?

   _____

2. What is your favorite play or musical ?

   _____

This Land Is Your Land

by Woody Guthrie

1. As I was walking
   That ribbon of highway
   I saw above me
   That endless skyway,
   I saw below me
   That golden valley.
   This land was made for you and me.

   Chorus:
   This land is your land,
   This land is my land,
   From California
   To the New York Island,
   From the redwood forest
   To the Gulf Stream waters;
   This land was made for you and me.

2. When the sun was shining
   And I was strolling
   And the wheat field waving
   And the dust clouds rolling
   As the fog was lifting
   A voice was chanting
   This land was made for you and me.

   Chorus

Write a new chorus.

Write words that fit your own town or country.

Georgia on my Mind

Words by Stuart Gorrell, music by Hoagy Carmichael

1. Georgia, Georgia, the whole day through
   Just an old sweet song
   Keeps Georgia on my mind,
   (Georgia on my mind . . .)

2. Each day, Georgia, a song of you
   Comes as sweet and clear
   As moonlight through the pines.

3. Other arms reach out to me,
   Other eyes smile tenderly,
   Still in peaceful dreams I see
   The road leads back to you.

4. Georgia, Georgia, no peace I find,
   Just an old sweet song
   Keeps Georgia on my mind,
   (Georgia on my mind . . .)

A. Make questions.

1. What _____ ?
   The singer is listening to a song.

2. When _____ ?
   There is moonlight at night.

3. Where _____ ?
   The road leads back to you.

B. Answer the questions.

Which is your favorite verse of the song? _____

Why? _____

Mail Myself to You

by Woody Guthrie

Chorus:
I'm gonna wrap myself in paper,
I'm gonna daub myself with glue,
Stick some stamps on top of my head;
I'm gonna mail myself to you.

1. I'm gonna tie me up in a red string.
   I'm gonna tie blue ribbons too.
   I'm gonna climb up in my mailbox;
   I'm gonna mail myself to you.
   Chorus

2. When you see me in your mailbox,
   Cut the string and let me out;
   Wash the glue off my fingers,
   Stick some bubble gum in my mouth.
   Chorus

3. Take me out of my wrapping paper,
   Wash the stamps off my head;
   Pour me full of ice cream sodas,
   Put me in my nice warm bed.
   Chorus

Find words in the song.

1. The word "gonna" is how the words sound.
   The two words are really: _____ _____

2. You sleep in a _____ .

3. To mail a letter, you have to put a _____ on it.

4. Then you put it in the _____ .

Unit Test Answers

Test 1

A. 1. My name is (student name). 2. Glad to meet you. 3. So long./See you later.

B. 1. Yes, it is. 2. No, it isn't. 3. It's a tie. 4. It's a jacket.

C. 1. This 2. That

D. 1. your   2. Thanks.

Test 2

A. 1. d   2. e   3. b   4. c   5. a

B. 1. is 2. It 3. are 4. are 5. They 6. I am

C. ten, seven, twenty, eight, eleven, fifteen

Test 3

A. 1. are 2. is 3. are 4. are

B. 1. It's on the table. 2. It's under the table. 3. She's on the bed. 4. She's behind the chair.

C. It's three o'clock. 2. It's three thirty./It's half past three. 3. It's quarter to four.

Test 4

A. 1. Who's this? 2. How old is she? 3. What color is her hair? 4. Is she thin or chubby? 5. What color are her eyes?

B. 1. Is he tall or short? 2. What's he wearing? 3. What's his name?

C. 1. Do you like carrots? 2. Do you like oranges?

D. 1. Can I help you? 2. Here you are. 3. Anything else? 4. Is that all?

Test 5

A. 1. eating 2. reading 3. on 4. drinking

B. 1. an 2. — 3. an 4. a

C. 1. How many boys are there? 2. How many guitars are there? 3. How many lamps are there? 4. How many chairs are there? 5. How many tables are there?

Test 6

A. 1. Are you (accept any nationality)? 2. Are you (accept any age)? 3. What's your occupation? 4. How long are you staying?

B. 1. How many babies are there? 2. How many cemeteries are there? 3. How many churches are there? 4. How many women are there?

C. is, in, far, are, to, there, many, at, in, in, of, on, front, is, no, and

Test 7

A. 1. brother 2. sister 3. father 4. mother 5. grandfather

B. 1. eye 2. ear 3. tooth 4. head 5. nose 6. throat

C. 1. c 2. d 3. e 4. f 5. a 6. b

Test 8

A. 1. Whose cup is this? 2. Whose glasses are these? 3. Which car is Jack's? 4. Which bike is Jack's?

B. 1. These 2. This 3. Those 4. This

C. 1. am, me 2. is, him 3. is, her 4. are, them 5. are, us

Test 9

A. 1. It's eleven-fifteen. It's quarter past eleven. 2. It's twelve thirty. It's half past twelve. 3. It's one forty-five. It's quarter to two.

B. 1. She's going to mail a letter. 2. They are going to take a train to (New York). 3. I am going to deposit some money. 4. We are going to visit a friend. 5. He's going to study. (Or accept other reasonable responses.)

C. 1. Where are you going? 2. Who's going with you? 3. When are you going?

Test 10

A. 1. walk 2. fly 3. run fast

B. 1. have 2. has 3. have 4. have

C. 1. It's snowing. 2. It's raining. 3. It's sunny.

D. February, April, June, August, October, December

Unit 1

Page 1

1. My name is Mary. 2. Good morning.
3. Glad to meet you. 4. Hello Lucy *or*
Hi! 5. Her name is Sue. 6. So long. 7.
His name is Don. 8. Pleased to meet
you, Sally.

Page 2

Part A
1. Yes, it is. 2. No, it isn't. 3. No, it isn't.
4. No, it isn't. 5. Yes, it is.
6. Yes, it is. 7. No, it isn't. 8. (student's
name)

Part B
1. What's your name? 2. Is his name
Peter? 3. What's his name? 4. What's
her name? 5. Is his name Peter?/Is her
name Mary? 6. Is his name Mike?/Is her
name Sue? 7. What's his name?

Page 3

Page 4

Part A
1. Yes, it is. 2. No, it isn't. 3. Yes, it is.
4. No, it isn't. 5. No, it isn't. 6. No, it isn't.
7. No, it isn't. 8. No, it isn't. 9. Yes, it is.
10. Yes, it is. 11. No, it isn't. 12. No, it
isn't.

Part B

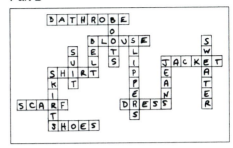

Page 5

1. b) Glad to meet you. 2. c) Good-bye.
3. b) her 4. a) his 5. a) Nunez 6. a)
Henry 7. b) It's a bathrobe. 8. c) You're
welcome.

Page 6

Part B
Accept any reasonable responses.

Unit 2

Page 7

Part A
1. Excuse me, is this your hat? 2. What's
your favorite color? 3. What color are his
shoes? 4. What's this? 5. What's she
wearing? 6. What's he wearing?

Part B
1. It's (color name). 2. They're/They are
(color name). 3. It's (color name). 4.
They're/They are (color name).

Page 8

Part A
1. later 2. raincoat 3. Betty 4. his 5.
please 6. this 7. it 8. red

Part B
1. Don 2. Peter 3. yes 4. name 5. Mary
6. hi 7. she 8. wearing 9. white 10.
glasses

Page 9

Part A
1. Yes, he is. 2. No, she isn't. 3. No, he
isn't. 4. Yes, she is. 5. Yes, he is. 6. No,
he isn't. 7. Yes, she is. 8. No, she isn't.

Part B
1. Tom is. 2. Don is. 3. Miguel is. 4. Mary is. 5. Rosa is. 6. Rosa is. 7. Tom is. 8. Miguel is.

Page 10

Part A
1. They are watching TV. 2. He is sleeping. 3. They are playing football. 4. He is singing. 5. They are dancing.

Part B
Accept any reasonable response.

Page 11

Part A

1. a hat	1. a tie
2. a blouse	2. a shirt
3. a sweater	3. a jacket
4. a raincoat	4. shorts
5. a skirt	5. socks
6. boots	6. shoes
7. glasses	

Part B
1. Her name is (accept any reasonable response). 2. What's his name? 3. Is his name 4. It's 5. it's not 6. Who is (Who's) 7. Is she wearing 8. How old 9. Thank you 10. thank you

Page 12

a) Nice to see you. b) How are you? a) Great! And you? b) Fine, just fine. a) That's good. b) Are you free later? a) Yes, I am. What time? b) At five o'clock. a) OK. Where do you want to meet? a) How about the cafeteria? b) Great! We can eat dinner. b) That sounds terrific. a) I'll see you at five o'clock!

Unit 3

Page 13

1. Where's Mary? 2. Is your name Lucy? 3. What's your name? 4. Where's Tom? 5. What color is the sofa? 6. Is this a shirt? 7. Where are my shoes? 8. Where's the lamp? 9. What's this? 10. Where's the rug?

Page 14

Part A
1. on 2. on 3. in front of 4. behind 5. under 6. in front of

Part B
1. It's on the bed. 2. It's on the table. 3. She's in front of the sofa. 4. They're behind the chair. 5. They're under the rug. 6. He's in front of the bus.

Page 15

Part A
1. It's three o'clock. 2. It's ten-thirty. 3. It's two-thirty. 4. It's eight-thirty. 5. It's quarter to five. 6. It's noon. 7. It's quarter past eight. 8. It's nine o'clock. 9. It's seven o'clock. 10. It's midnight. 11. It's five o'clock. 12. It's quarter to seven.

Part B

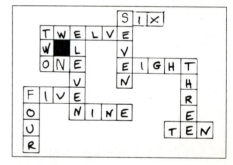

Page 16

Good morning/Pleased to meet you, Miss Black/Glad to meet you/
What time /two-thirty/is the next bus?/I don't know

Page 17

Part A
1. in 2. on 3. in 4. on 5. on

Part B
1. b 2. a 3. c 4. c 5. c

Page 18

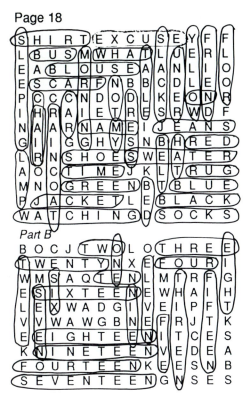

Part B

Unit 4

Page 19

Part A

Hi/Where?/that's/It's/He's

Part B

Hello, Mike./Hi, Betty./that girl?/Who?/in the hat./Sally./her last name?/Smith./she your girl friend?/No, she isn't.

Page 20

1. No, it's black. 2. No, she's chubby. 3. Yes, he is. 4. No, she's eighteen. 5. He's thirty-two. 6. No, he's thin. 7. Yes, it is. 8. She's nineteen. 9. She's wearing a hat. 10. He's wearing a sweater.

Page 21

Part A

Sam, His, He, tall, He, thirty-three, He, black, white, white, His, black, black

Part B

Accept any reasonable response.

Page 22

Part A

1. It's an apple. 2. It's a peach. 3. It's a banana. 4. It's a carrot. 5. It's a pear. 6. It's an egg. 7. It's a sandwich. 8. It's a candy bar.

Part B

1. It's on the floor. 2. They're under the chair. 3. They're on the table. 4. It's under the sofa. 5. He's behind the chair.

Page 23

Part A

1. It's Bill. 2. He's twenty. 3. What color is his hair? 4. He's thin.

Part B

1. What color are her eyes? 2. What's her first name? 3. What's her last name? 4. How old is she? 5. Is she chubby or thin? 6. What color is her hair? 7. Is she short or tall?

Page 24

Hello, waitress, newspaper, name, job, at, telephone, you

Unit 5

Page 25

Part A

1. She's eating an egg. 2. She's eating a peach. 3. She's eating an orange. 4. She's eating a carrot.

Part B

1. He's buying a fish. 2. He's drinking coffee. 3. He's eating ice cream. 4. He's eating meat. 5. He's sitting in the (an) armchair. 6. He's reading a book. 7. He's drinking tea. 8. He's buying carrots.

Page 26

Part A

1. What's her last name? 2. What color is it? 3. What's this? 4. What's she like? 5. What's his name? 6. What's she wearing? 7. What's her name? 8. What's he wearing?

Part B

1. Is he eating an apple? 2. Who's wearing a blue dress? 3. Is this her book? 4. Who's wearing slacks? 5. Is this your tie? 6. Is he eating an apple?

Page 27

Part A

1. She's eating an apple. 2. He's reading a newspaper. 3. She's drinking coffee. 4. She's sitting in the (a) bathtub. 5. He's reading a book. 6. She's buying eggs. 7. She's drinking lemonade.

Part B

Mary is in her room. She's sitting on the bed. She's eating a pear. She's drinking tea. She's reading a comic book.

Page 28

Part A

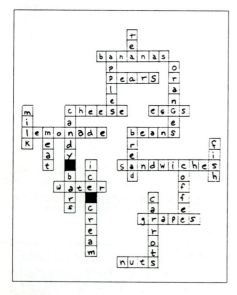

Part B

1. meat 2. purple 3. dollars 4. pears 5. eggs 6. ice cream

Page 29

Part A

1. a 2. b 3. b 4. b 5. b 6. a 7. b

Part B

carrots, bread, cheese, grapes, meat, apples

Page 30

1. on the eighth floor 2. on the first floor 3. on the sixth floor 4. on the second floor 5. on the tenth floor 6. on the fourth floor 7. on the third floor 8. on the ninth floor 9. on the fifth floor 10. on the seventh floor

Unit 6

Page 31

Part A

1. How are you? 2. Is your name Tom? 3. What's your nationality? 4. How old are you? 5. What's your name? 6. Are you still a secretary? 7. Are you a doctor? *or* Are you a waiter? 8. Are you a waiter? *or* Are you a doctor?

Part B

Accept any reasonable responses.

Page 32

1. She's a nurse 2. She's a chef 3. She's an architect 4. He's a student. 5. He's an army officer. 6. She's a doctor. 7. He's a football player. 8. He's a waiter. 9. He's a taxi driver. 10. She's a flight attendant. 11. He's a teacher. 12. She's a pilot.

Page 33

1. His name is Frank. 2. He's fine. 3. He's Brazilian. 4. He's a student. 5. It's black. 6. She's his sister. 7. She's a nurse. 8. She's twenty-two. 9. She's listening to records. 10. No, he's short and chubby. 11. He's in the armchair. 12. Her name is Pat. 13. Yes, they are. 14. No, they're not.

Page 34

1. There is one car. There are two cars. 2. There are two churches. There is one church. 3. There are five oranges. There is one orange. 4. There are two bridges. There is one bridge. 5. There are four children. There is one child. 6. There are six women. There is one woman.

Page 35

Part A
1. — 2. — 3. a 4. an 5. an 6. a

Part B
1. Carmen 2. Mexican 3. doctor 4. his nationality 5. How old is he? 6. accountant 7. pilot 8. What's his nationality

Page 36

Accept any reasonable responses.

Unit 7

Page 37

Page 38

Part A
1. aunt 2. brother 3. grandmother 4. mother 5. cousin 6. sister 7. uncle 8. grandfather 9. father

Part B
1. library 2. concert 3. soccer game 4. theater 5. church 6. supermarket

Page 39

Part A
1. My ears hurt./I have a bad ear. 2. My arm hurts./I have a bad arm. 3. They have bad legs./Their legs hurt. 4. His tooth hurts./He has a bad tooth.

Part B
toe / foot / head / knee /
ankle / arm / hip / leg /
stomach / finger

Page 40

Part A
1. are 2. is 3. are 4. is 5. am 6. are

Part B
1. What are you eating? 2. What's (What is) she doing? 3. What are we/you buying? 4. What are they eating? 5. Who is Susie? 6. What's (What is) he reading? 7. Where is she? 8. What's (What is) his occupation? 9. What are you doing? 10. What are they buying?

Page 41

Part A
1. are 2. are 3. He 4. am 5. are 6. They

Part B
1. son 2. daughter 3. wife 4. sister 5. parents

Page 42

Accept any reasonable responses.

Unit 8

Page 43

1. These books are Tom's. 2. That car is Mary's. 3. These shoes are Jill's. 4. That hat is Fred's. 5. These ties are Tom's. 6. This bathrobe is Jack's. 7. Those boots are Peter's. 8. Those glasses are Lucy's. 9. That ice cream is Pat's. 10. This guitar is Mike's.

Page 44

Part A

1. Jack is helping me 2. Jack is helping you 3. Jack is helping us 4. Jack is helping them 5. Jack is helping her 6. Jack is helping him

Part B

1. Give it to her. 2. Give it to him. 3. Give it to them. 4. Give it to her. 5. Give it to us. 6. Give it to me.

Page 45

1. Yes, it is. Give it to me, please. 2. Yes, they are. Give them to me, please. 3. Yes, it is. Give it to her, please. 4. Yes, it is. Give it to me, please. 5. Yes, they are. Give them to him, please. 6. Yes, it is. Give it to him, please. 7. Yes, they are. Give them to me, please. 8. Yes, it is. Give it to her, please. 9. Yes, it is. Give it to him, please. 10. Yes, they are. Give them to me, please.

Page 46

Part A

1. kitchen 2. hats 3. parents 4. friend 5. him 6. garage 7. carrots 8. the Greens' 9. sandwiches 10. sons

Part B

1. car 2. church 3. airport 4. roller skates 5. bridge 6. newspaper 7. records 8. racket 9. guitar

Page 47

Part A

1. b 2. a 3. b 4. a 5. a

Part B

1. those 2. that 3. those 4. those 5. This 6. Those 7. these 8. These/those

Page 48

Possible answers: 1. Take Route 405 (south) and then take take Route 42 (east). 2. Take Route 710 (south) to Route 91 (west) to Sepulveda Blvd. 3. Take Route 10 (east) to Route 405 (south) and then take Route 42 (east). 4. Take Route 7 (north) to Route 710 (north). Accept other reasonable responses.

Unit 9

Page 49

Part A

1. It's ten-fifteen (10:15). 2. It's nine-thirty (9:30). 3. It's four o'clock (4:00). 4. It's four-forty-five (4:45).

Part B

1. Mary is going in the morning. 2. Reynaldo is coming in the afternoon. 3. John is going in the evening. 4. The party is at night. 5. The train is coming at noon. 6. Gloria is singing at midnight.

Page 50

Part A

1. She's going to the supermarket. 2. He's going to the bus station. 3. They're going to the theater. 4. I'm going to the airport. 5. She's going to the library. 6. He's going to the train station. 7. We're going to the bank. 8. They're going to the post office.

Part B

1. airport 2. police station 3. bus station 4. library 5. post office 6. supermarket 7. train station 8. theater 9. bank

Page 51

Part A

1. I'm going to London. My mother is. At half past seven. 2. I'm going to a party. My cousin is. At eight-fifteen. 3. I'm going to the museum. My aunt is. At ten-twenty.

Part B

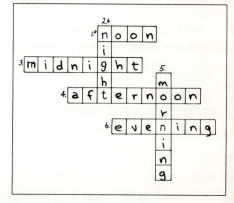

Page 52

Part A

How, Just, What, watching, is, go, so long, later

Part B

at, reading, in, on, reading, listening, living, sandwiches, is going, record, watch, has to

Page 53

Part A

1. Whose 2. Whose /they're 3. them to him 4. it to me 5. Where are you going? 6. When are you going 7. Are you 8. Who's going with you?

Part B

1. two-fifteen 2. eight twenty-five 3. one-thirty (half past one) 4. twenty to three

Page 54

Accept any reasonable responses.

Unit 10

Page 55

1. No, I'm sorry. I have to wash the dishes. 2. No, I'm sorry. He has to wash the window(s). 3. No, I'm sorry. She has to type a letter. 4. No, I'm sorry. They have to wash the car. 5. No, I'm sorry. I have to study. 6. No, I'm sorry. They have to brush the dog. 7. No, I'm sorry. She has to go to the supermarket.

Page 56

Part A

1. No, he can't. 2. Yes, she can. 3. Yes, they can. 4. No, they can't. 5. Yes, he can. 6. No, they can't. 7. No, she can't.

Part B

Accept any reasonable responses.

Page 57

Part A

1. Tuesday 2. Thursday 3. Sunday 4. Monday 5. Saturday 6. Wednesday 7. Friday

Part B

1. fall 2. summer 3. spring 4. fall 5. summer 6. winter 7. spring 8. winter 9. summer 10. spring 11. fall 12. winter

Page 58

Part A

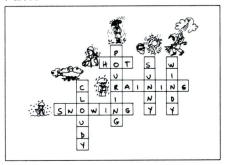

Part B

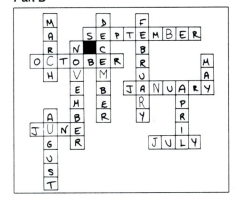

Page 59

Part A

1. b 2. c 3. c 4. c

Part B

1. are they watching 2. are we going 3. many babies 4. two men, men 5. women 6. libraries 7. we are both tall 8. so am, you are both handsome

Page 60

Part A

1. bad cough, is, medicine, it, day 2. toothache, pills 3. lotion, four 4. Eat, meals 5. knee, exercise

Part B

Accept any reasonable responses.

PRONOUNS

PERSONAL PRONOUNS (Units 2, 6, 7)

I am eighteen.

			We
He		chubby.	**You** are friends.
She	is	handsome.	**They**
It		at home.	

OBJECT PRONOUNS (Unit 8)

Give the book to **me**.
Tom is helping **me/you/him/her/us/them**.

DEMONSTRATIVE PRONOUNS (Units 1, 8)

This is her hat.   **That** is his hat.
These are cars.   **Those** are cars.

ADJECTIVES

ADJECTIVE + NOUN (Unit 2)

Bill is wearing a **red** shirt.   I'm wearing my **new** blouse.

PREDICATE ADJECTIVES (Units 4, 6)

The weather is **sunny**.   We are **tired**.

You're **handsome** and **so** is your friend.
You are **both handsome**.

POSSESSIVE ADJECTIVES (Units 1, 8)

	my			
	your		**Our**	
This is	**his**	friend.	**Your**	dog is very big.
	her		**Their**	

DEMONSTRATIVE ADJECTIVES (Unit 8)

This car is red.   **That** car is green.
These cars are old.   **Those** cars are new.

PREPOSITIONS OF PLACE/TIME (Units 3, 10)

The tie is	**on** **under**	the chair.	Don is **at** the bus stop.
Mr. Jones is	**in front of** **behind**	Mrs. Rivera.	Lucy is **in** the bedroom.

They're coming **on** Friday. I'm going **in** May. I'm eating **at** eight.

CONJUNCTIONS (Units 4, 6, 8)

He's very tall **and** handsome. There are four buses **but** one train.
I am tired, **so** Jack is helping me.

NOUNS

NOUN PLURALS (Units 5, 6)

Regular:	bank	orange	bus	country	church
	bank**s**	orange**s**	bus**es**	countr**ies**	church**es**
Irregular:	child	man	woman	foot	tooth
	child**ren**	**men**	wom**en**	**feet**	**teeth**

COUNT NOUNS/MASS NOUNS (Unit 5)

He's eating **a pear/pears**.　　　　He's eating **an apple/apples**.

He's eating **fish**.　　　　He's drinking **tea**.

POSSESSIVE OF NOUNS (Unit 8)

		the boys'/the Browns'.
Whose shirt is this?	It's	**Jack's/Bess's**.

DEFINITE ARTICLE the, INDEFINITE ARTICLES a and an, NO ARTICLE (Units 3, 5)

The tie is on **the** table.　　　　He's drinking tea.
He's eating **a** pear.　　　　He's eating pears.
He's eating **an** apple.　　　　He's eating apples.

CONTRACTIONS (Units 1, 2, 3, 10)

I am—**I'm**	he/she is—**he's/she's**	we are—**we're**
you are—**you're**	it is—**it's**	they are—**they're**
what is—**what's**	that is—**that's**	where is—**where's**
who is—**who's**	is not—**isn't**　are not—**aren't**	can not—**can't**

VERBS

SIMPLE PRESENT **to be** (Units 1, 2, 3, 6)

I **am** Elena Silva.
You **are** a nurse.
He/She **is** an accountant.
It **is** cold.

We
You   **are** happy.
They

to be + PREDICATE ADJECTIVE/NOUN (Units 4, 6)

I **am tall**.   He **is Japanese**.
She **is a doctor**.

His hair **is black**.
They **are teachers**.

PRESENT PROGRESSIVE (Units 5, 7)

I **am going** to the supermarket.
You **are buying** bread.
He **is drinking** coffee.
She **is reading** a book.
It **is raining**.

We **are sitting** in the kitchen.
You **are watching** television.
They **are dancing**.

PRESENT PROGRESSIVE IN FUTURE SENSE (Unit 9)

When **are** you **going**? Tomorrow.

PRESENT PROGRESSIVE CONTRASTED WITH SIMPLE PRESENT (Unit 5)

Dick **is** in his room.

He**'s sitting** on the bed.

CAN (ABILITY/PERMISSION) (Unit 10)

I **can** swim.
Can you make coffee?
Mom, **can** I go to the movies?

No, I **can't**.
Yes, you **can**.

HAVE TO/HAS TO (Unit 10)

I/You/We/They **have to** go.

He/She **has to** go.

THERE IS/THERE ARE (Unit 6)

There is one train station.
Is there one library?

There are two bus stations.
Are there two banks?

STATEMENTS (Unit 1)

His name is Tom. It's Tom.
Joe is wearing a blue hat.

QUESTIONS

YES-NO QUESTIONS (Units 1, 2)

Is his name Tom?

INFORMATION QUESTIONS-QUESTION WORDS (Units 1, 2, 3)

Where are you going?
What is he doing?
Who is going with you?
When are they coming?
Which room is she in?
How old is he?
How many lamps are there?
Whose cup is this?

Where's the tie?
What's the weather like?
Who's this?
When's the next bus?

CHOICE QUESTIONS (Unit 2)

Is he wearing a blue hat, **or** a red hat?

SHORT ANSWERS (Unit 6)

Yes, I am. No, I'm not.
Yes, you are. No, you're not.
Yes, s(he) is. No, s(he) isn't.

Yes, it is. No, it isn't.
Yes, we are. No, we aren't.
Yes, they are. No, they aren't.

TIME STRUCTURES

PHRASES (Unit 9)

I'm going
in the afternoon/morning/evening.
at midnight/noon/night.
this morning/afternoon.
today/tonight/tomorrow/now.

It's **ten-twenty** (10:20).
It's **ten-thirty** (10:30).

TIME QUESTIONS (Unit 3)

What time is it?
When is the next bus?

AURAL/ORAL LANGUAGE

Listening Comprehension

Understanding basic structures/vocabulary/
expressions

Understanding and responding to questions

Understanding and responding to spoken
narratives

Matching spoken words, sentences, descriptions
to pictures

Oral Communication

Inquiring/Reporting:

clothing/colors

ownership

names/ages

what people are doing

quantity/cost

location of things/people

time structures/phrases

food/drink; likes/dislikes

physical characteristics/health

occupations

family members/relationships

future intention/destinations

climate/weather

ability/knowledge

Describing/Identifying:

number names, colors

people

household furniture/rooms

nationalities

body parts/illness

sports/games/skills

days/months/year/seasons

Social/Life Skills:

Greeting/introducing/taking leave

Agreeing/disagreeing/correcting

	1	2	3	4	5	6	7	8	9	10

Apologizing

Giving/receiving gifts

Taking a bus

Asking for/giving directions

Making change

Buying groceries/clothing/tickets

Eating with family/friends

Using a library

Discussing health

Expressing sympathy

Giving/seeking/denying permission

Role playing fixed and free dialogues

Following conversational sequence

Playing language games

Pronunciation

Focusing on sentence intonation/word stress

Discriminating among and practicing:

    [-s], [-z], [-iz] sounds

    other consonant sounds

    other vowel sounds

Practicing rhythm, stress, intonation in

    poems/songs

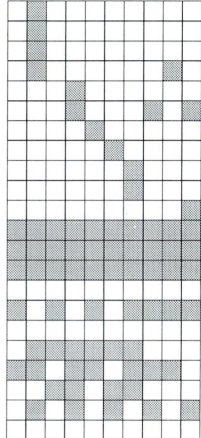

LITERATURE AND CULTURAL AWARENESS

Learning language through poems/songs

Recognizing rhyme, rhythm

Learning about life/culture of the U.S.

READING AND WRITING

Reading Skills

Participating in shared reading

Developing compehension skills:

    Answering questions/recalling details

    Relating fiction/nonfiction to own experience

Developing basic sight vocabulary

Reading sentences and dialogues

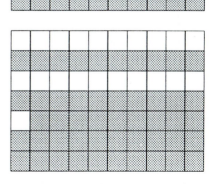

Writing Skills

Writing all letters/numerals to 100

Spelling known words correctly

Writing words/sentences/paragraphs/dialogues

Writing dictation

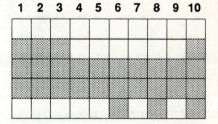

GRAMMAR/STRUCTURES

Simple statements

Yes/No questions and answers

Information questions

Alternative questions

Short answers

Articles: a/an, the

Count/mass/plural nouns

Possessive nouns/pronouns

Demonstrative adjectives/pronouns

Descriptive adjectives

Prepositions

There is/are

Numbers (cardinal/ordinal)

Contractions

Verbs

    Present tense: to be

    Present tense: to have

    Present progressive

    Future: going to

    Commands

Modals: do/don't, can/can't, has to/have to

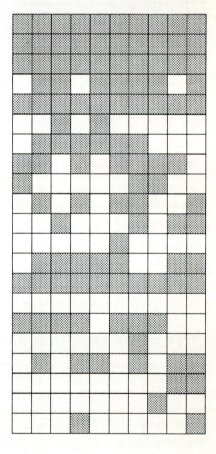

Word List

a 16
adults 116
a lot of 111
about 61
accountant 62
after 10
afternoon 103
age 64
airport(s) 65
all 73
am 61
an 50
and 39
ankle 76
Anything else? 43
apple(s) 41
architect 62
Are there any . . . nearby?
    104
Are you sure . . . ? 109
are 15
arm 76
armchair 29
army officer 62
at 31
at home 79
aunt 102
average 92
awful 76

baby(ies) 65
back 76
backache 74
bad 74
banana(s) 50
bank(s) 65
bathrobe 6
bathroom 78
bathtub 29
be 109
beans 41
beautiful 92
bed 26
bedroom 25
before 10
behind 28
belt 6
big 86
bike 104
black 14

blond(e) 38
blouse 6
blue 14
book 44
boots 15
boy 39
boyfriend 39
bread 52
breakfast 113
bridge(s) 66
briefcase 8
brother(s) 74
brown 14
brush 111
brush(es) 66
buildings 67
bus 31
bus station 67
bus stop 31
but 67
butter 56
buy 100
buying 49
Bye. 3

calculator 44
can 109
Can I help you? 43
Can you change a dollar?
    32
Can you tell me . . . ? 104
candy bar(s) 41
cane 8
can't 109
car 29
card 68
carrot(s) 41
cat 29
cemetery(ies) 65
cent(s) 44
chair 25
change 112
check out 68
cheese 52
chef 62
chest 76
chicken 56
child 66
children 29
chubby 38

church(es) 66
circles 86
circus 116
clean 111
clothes 111
cloudy 114
coat 8
coffee 52
cold (n.) 74
cold 114
color 14
Come again soon. 8
Come in. 112
Come on over. 73
comic book 54
computer 109
computer game 79
concert 103
control 64
cooking (v.) 78
cooking 68
costume party 89
cough 74
country(ies) 65
cousin 102
cup 85

dance (n.) 103
dancing 19
daughter 74
day 67
dear 49
deposit 100
dinner 10
do 41
doctor 61
dog 49
doing 19
dollar(s) 43
dress 6
drinking 49
drinks 113
drive 110
driving 19
drizzling 114

ear 76
eating 49
egg(s) 42
elbow 76

magazine 44
mail 100
mall 104
man 39
many 67
math 109
me 90
meat 52
medium 92
men 66
midnight 30
milk 53
money 100
mother 74
movies 103
museum 103
music 68
my 1

name 2
napkin 56
nationality 64
nearby 104
neat 92
need 56
new 39
newspaper 44
next 31
Nice to meet you. 43
night 94
no 5
No, I'm not. 61
noise 67
noon 30
nose 76
not 29
Not bad. 61
Not so good. 76
notebook 44
now 30
nurse 62
nuts 41

occupation 64
(two) o'clock 30
office 88
Oh dear. 112
Oh no it isn't! 13
on 25
only 67

or 18
orange 14
oranges 41
other 67
our 73
over there 37
owner 43

package 100
pants 37
parents 74
party 103
pass 56
passengers 101
passport 64
peach(es) 41
pear(s) 42
pen 8
pencil 87
people 67
pepper 56
petite 92
pick up 101
pilot 62
pizza 56
plane 97
play 101
player 86
playing 19
please 43
Pleased to meet you. 1
police station 67
polish 111
pollution 67
post office 67
pouring 114
pretty 39
programmer 109
public 104
purple 14
purse 8

quarter past six 30
quarter to ten 30

racket 86
radio(s) 55
raincoat 6
raining 114
read 112

reading 54
record(s) 55
red 14
restrooms 104
return 101
Right! 113
rock concert 112
roller skates 86
room 54
rug 27
run 110

salad 56
salt 56
sandwich(es) 41
scarf 6
school 105
second 104
secretary 62
See you later. 3
See you soon. 113
see 101
she 16
shirt 6
shoes 15
short 38
shorts 17
sign 112
sing 110
singing 19
sir 94
sister 74
sit 112
sitting 54
size 92
skate 110
ski 110
skirt 6
slacks 15
sleeping 19
slippers 15
small 67
snakes 68
snowing 114
start 116
So long. 1
so 90
soccer 116
socks 15
sofa 25

some 100
son 74
sore 80
Sorry 20
spaghetti 56
spoon 56
sports 68
spring 113
square 67
squares 86
start 116
staying 64
still 61
stomach 76
stomachache 74
Stop! 112
store 49
strawberry(ies) 65
student 61
study 111
sugar 56
suit 7
summer 113
sun 115
sunny 114
supermarket(s) 65
sweater 7

table 26
take 100
take out 68
taking 113
tall 38
taxi 97
taxi driver 62
tea 49
teacher 61
teeth 66
tennis 111
terrible 76
Thank you. 8
Thank you very much. 20
Thanks. 8
that 7
That's all. 64
That's right. 63
the 23

theater(s) 65
their 90
them 85
there 37
these 85
they 15
thin 38
third 104
this 1
This is perfect! 92
those 86
throat 76
thumb 76
tickets 116
tie 6
tired 90
to 90
today 103
toe 76
tomorrow 94
tonight 103
too 92
too sick 80
tooth 66
toothache 74
traffic 67
train 67
T-shirt 20
TV 19
type 109

ugly 92
uncle 102
under 25
us 90
use 109

vacation 113
very 39
village 67
visit 101

wait 112
waiter 62
waiting for 73
walk 110
wallet 8

want 68
warm 114
wash 111
washing 79
watching 19
water 52
we 29
wearing 16
weather 114
weeks 64
Well . . . 5
wet paint 112
What time is it? 30
what 2
What's (s)he like? 39
What's the matter
    with . . .? 76
What time is it? 30
when 31
where 25
which 78
white 14
who 18
whose 85
wife 74
windows 111
windy 114
winter 113
with 102
woman 37
women 66
work 80
wrist 76

yard 29
year 113
years old 74
yellow 14
yes 5
you 3
your 2
You're welcome 8

one–twenty 20
ten–hundred 32